To our long-standing intercontinental friendship

Elies

EUROPE AND ITS MEMBERS

If you will it is not a dream (....).
Dream and reality are not so far apart as is often thought.
All the acts of mankind were dreams once and will become dreams again.

Theodor Herzl, Altneuland (Old new land)

Europe and its Members

A Constitutional Approach

ELIES STEYGER

Dartmouth

Aldershot • Brookfield USA • Singapore • Sydney

Published by
Dartmouth Publishing Company Limited
Gower House
Croft Road
Aldershot
Hants GU11 3HR
England

Dartmouth Publishing Company
Old Post Road
Brookfield
Vermont 05036
USA

British Library Cataloguing in Publication Data
Steyger, Elies
Europe and Its Members: A Constitutional Approach
I. Title
341.2422

Library of Congress Cataloging-in-Publication Data
Steyger, Elies.
Europe and its members : a constitutional approach / by Elies Steyger.
p. cm.
Includes bibliographical references and index.
ISBN 1-85521-655-8
1. European Economic Community countries–Constitutional law.
2. International law and municipal law–European Economic Community countries. I. Title.
KJE5075.S74 1995
341.24'22–dc20 95-5684
CIP

Printed and bound in Great Britain by
Ipswich Book Co. Ltd., Ipswich, Suffolk

ISBN 1 85521 655 8

Contents

Acknowledgements

This book started out as a paper on the principle of subsidiarity, presented at the the annual meeting of the Law and Society Association in Chicago (1993). It was meant to end up as an article in some or the other law journal. While I was writing the paper, however, many of my friends and colleagues expressed interest in the subject. They convinced me that a book dealing with the constitutional relationship between the Community and its member states would be useful, not only for law students, but also for all those non-specialist lawyers who are forced to deal with the intricacies of Community law without precisely understanding where, how and for what reasons Community law interferes with other areas of the law. Through their encouragement I became confident enough to extend the subject of the original paper to the book you have before you. I would like to thank all of them.

My colleagues of the Department of legal and legislative affairs of the then Ministry of Social Services, Public Health and Cultural Affairs (WVC) of the Netherlands deserve special gratitude. Though they clearly felt that writing a book on legal issues in one's spare time was not a very sane thing to do, they never hesitated to lend their support. Special thanks should be extended to my colleague Lies Bakker who, probably without knowing it, contributed very much to this book by providing me with materials which, though seemingly unrelated to the subject at first sight, proved to be highly relevant in the end.

Since English is not my native language, the entire text had to be edited. One fax was enough to get Terry Morehead Dworkin (Indiana University, Bloomington, IN) to organize this within a few days. Craig

Douglas (Berkeley, CA), who made the actual corrections, worked quickly and precisely. That I felt compelled to retain some established 'Euro-English' jargon is not his fault, but one of the less palatable results of the ongoing European integration process. Other people too demonstrated such a 'that's what friends are for' attitude. Malva Driessen (University of Limburg) and Hans Zeijen (Social Security Appeals Court (CRvB)) were very helpful in providing me with materials I needed. Though they are employed elsewhere, one telephone call was usually enough to bring them to action.

Joel Paul (American University, Washington DC) provided me with comments on the original paper which improved the book as a whole. My father deserves thanks for taking care of the index, without which this book would not have been complete.

Nico Verheij (Ministry of Justice, The Netherlands) acted as a representative of the group of lawyers for whom this book is intended. He read through earlier drafts and provided me with comments which helped the book to acquire its final form. Not restricted to being an excellent lawyer, he also proved to be a computer wiz who was able to make the copy camera-ready. For all this I owe him a debt of gratitude. I am most grateful, however, for his unflagging support during the process of writing.

Finally, my daughter Tamar contributed to the whole thing in her own way. Thoroughly unimpressed with my writing, she took my mind off 'Europe....' by claiming my attention for more pleasant things such as going to the movies or hiking in the Ardennes. In the end these diversions did more for this book than she will ever know.

The law is stated as it stands on January 1st, 1995.

Elies Steyger
The Hague, December 1994

Abbreviations

AA	Ars Aequi
AB	Administratiefrechtelijke beslissingen (Dutch Court Reports, Administrative Law)
AELE	Association Européenne de libre échange
A-G	Advocate-General
CBB	College van Beroep voor het Bedrijfsleven (Economic Appeals Court) (The Netherlands)
CRvB	Centrale Raad van Beroep (Social Security Appeals Court) (The Netherlands)
CLMRev	Common Market Law Review
Dir.	Directive
EC	European Communities
ECHR	European Convention on the Protection of Human Rights and Fundamental Freedoms
ECR	European Court Reports
ECSC	European Coal and Steel Community
EEC	European Economic Community
EFTA	European Free Trade Association
EIB	European Institute of Public Administration (EIPA)
ELR	European Law Review
EuR	Europäisches Recht
HR	Hoge Raad der Nederlanden (Supreme Court of the Netherlands)
ICJ	International Court of Justice
JCMSt	Journal of Common Market Studies

JO	Journal Officiel de la Communauté Européenne
LIEI	Legal Issues of European Integration
NJ	Nederlandse Jurisprudentie (Dutch Court Reports)
NJB	Nederlands Juristenblad
NTB	Nederlands Tijdschrift voor Bestuursrecht
nyr	not yet reported
OJ	Official Journal of the European Community
OOPEC	Office for Official Publications of the European Community
Reg.	Regulation
Res.	Resolution
RM Themis	Rechtsgeleerd Magazijn Themis
SEW	Sociaal Economische Wetgeving
SMA	Sociaal Maandblad Arbeid
Trb	Tractatenblad (Official Journal on Treaties in the Netherlands)

I The F-word

Federal elements in the relationship between the Community and its members

1 Introduction

In 1957, six European governments concluded the Treaty establishing the EEC (the Treaty).[1] With this act they embarked on a voyage the destination of which could not be predicted. Though the Community started with six participants, within a few years it became apparent that there was a seventh companion, a seventh who would not go away anymore. This seventh participant turned out to be the Community itself.

The EEC turned out to be more than a vehicle for co-operation between the member states. The new Community government, explicitly established by the Treaty itself and more implicitly created by the supranational structure of the Treaty, turned out to be a major influence in the European integration process: an influence to be reckoned with in the future. The independent existence of the Community Institutions as a government has been a continuing source of interest for researchers and politicians.

But the question remains: what is the Community? The Community exists and is here to stay, that much is certain. It has a government and it has the ability to impose certain rules on its members and their citizens. But is it a State? A Federation? Something else?

The question of the nature of the Community has not yet been solved. Some participants in the debate maintain that the Community must be seen as a federation-to-be, as a state in the making.[2] Others are adamant that the Community is a confederation, an international organization in which the members retain their own identity and keep their destiny in their own hands.[3] Still others feel the Community is something entirely different and does not fit the old classifications.[4]

Also, within the Community different views are held about where the Community should be heading. This has been the case since the sixties when France decided it could not accept those Community decisions it had voted against.[5] In the eighties the European Parliament drafted a Treaty establishing a European Union[6] in which many federal elements were incorporated.[7] This draft treaty was never adopted; the less radical Single European Act,[8] which modified the Treaty establishing the EEC, was adopted instead.[9]

During the Intergovernmental Conference of 1991 the Dutch chair of the Council also proposed a modification of the Treaty with strong federal features. This proposal was rejected unanimously by the other member states. The negotiations during the Conference of 1991 eventually led to the much more moderate Treaty of Maastricht.[10]

The Treaty of Maastricht in turn led to disputes about the question whether the Community had a future as a federation or a confederation. These disputes culminated in a judgment by the German Constitutional Court in which it ruled that the German Republic is under an obligation to withdraw from the Community if the principle of democracy in the German Constitution is violated by the ongoing European integration.[11] The German Court felt this could happen if Germany would confer sovereign powers to the Community not limited by the Treaty.

At this point in time it therefore remains to be seen whether the Community is one day going to be a federation or not. Though even the original Treaty establishing the EEC already contained federal elements, the Community still lacks powers which are characteristic of well-known federations like Germany or the United States of America. For example, the Community lacks exclusive powers in the areas of foreign policy or defence.

Nevertheless, since its establishment the Community has gained enormous powers over its members. There are very few national policy areas in which national legislators can regulate without having to reckon with the limits the Community has set over the years.

This influence is very much due to the legal aspects of European integration. The Court of Justice has used its powers to interpret the provisions of the Treaty and secondary law in such a way that member states and their citizens could not fail to notice the effects of EC law in their daily lives. So although it started as just another treaty under international law, where the relationship between Community and its members is concerned the Treaty now resembles a constitution.

The constitutional elements of the Treaty were reinforced after the adoption of the Single European Act in 1987. This Treaty added to the already existing powers of the Community. The Treaty of Maastricht also adds a constitutional element by introducing the principle of subsidiarity in the relationship between the Community and its members.[12] This principle will govern the use of powers by the Community in those areas where regulating powers are shared by the member states and the Community.

These constitutional elements will form the main focus of this book. The author intends to place them within the context of the relationship between the Community and the member states. How are powers divided between the Community and its members? Which powers still belong exclusively to the member states? What are the limits the member states have to take into account when establishing their national policies? What are the limits the Community has to respect when regulating large parts of the policy areas which originally belonged to the exclusive jurisdiction of the member states?

To answer these questions, several issues have to be dealt with. First the distribution of powers within the Community and the transfer of powers to the Community will be examined (chapter two). Then the focus will be on the possible influence of the principle of subsidiarity (chapter three). After that the author will narrow the scope of her inquiries to take a look at the most peculiar feature of Community law, the legislative device of the directive and its effects on the freedom of the member states to conduct their policy with the means they consider the most appropriate (chapter four). Finally the author will summarize her conclusions (chapter five).

At first, however, the focus will be on the federal elements in the Treaty itself and on the way the Court of Justice turned the Treaty into a constitution instead of an ordinary treaty.

Two things remain to be said. First, the Treaty of Maastricht which altered the Treaties establishing the ECSC, the EEC and Euratom in many ways, also caused some confusion concerning the names of the different Community institutions and the entity as a whole. It is not yet clear whether the Community should be named Union or not. In this book the word 'Community' is used if only the entity which acts within the supranational part of the Treaties (i.e. EC, Euratom and ECSC) is meant. The word Union is reserved for the entity which acts within the Treaty of Maastricht as a whole including the intergovernmental parts of that Treaty.

Secondly, this book is not an introduction to the law of the European Communities. The reader is assumed to have a basic knowledge of Community law. Discussion of the basics of Community law will be kept as short as possible.

2 Federal elements in Community law

The Treaty as it was adopted in the fifties already contained elements alien to most other treaties.[13] Among these federal elements is article 5 EEC-Treaty and the way it is used in the Community context. Article 5 contains an explicit obligation for the member states to comply with Community law and to abstain from adopting measures interfering with the purpose or the effects of Community law. This means the member states are not allowed to take any measure which may jeopardize the operation of any Community measure. Though this principle is directly derived from international law,[14] in Community law the Court of Justice is empowered to interpret this principle and examine national measures in the light of this principle.[15]

Also, the Treaty provides the Community with powers to legislate on several subjects if the majority of the member states vote in favour of the legislative measure. Another federal element is the jurisdiction of the Court of Justice of the European Community. The interpretation of Community law is a power of the Court, which is an independent institution, not of the judges of the member states. Another significant element is that certain Treaty provisions directly address individuals, bypassing the member states.

These elements were not exactly novelties in 1957. By then the ECSC[16] had already been in existence for five years. From that treaty most of these federal elements were derived. The scope of the treaty establishing the ECSC is, however, very limited compared to the Treaty establishing the EEC. In that respect the adoption of far-reaching federal elements in a Treaty with a much more undefined scope may be regarded as revolutionary indeed. In later years the Court of Justice added to this federal character of the Treaty by providing Community citizens with the ability to rely directly on Community law.

While the member states consciously adopted these constitutional elements in the fifties, they apparently did not always realize what they had gotten themselves into. Majority voting in the Council of Ministers was not achieved without some political fights. Also, the judgments of the Court of Justice which considerably strengthened the federal character of the Treaty often shocked the member states to the bone. Negotiations on alterations in the Treaty, usually started in order to reinforce the Community as an organization, were sometimes used by the member states to limit the consequences of the judgments of the Court.[17]

Before describing these sometimes contradictory movements of the member states and the Community institutions in the next chapter it is necessary to first discuss the institutional structure and the legal order of the Community. These elements form the foundation of the constitutional character of the Treaty.

2.1 *The structure of the Community institutions established by the Treaty*

The European Community as an organization was established in the fifties in the three treaties establishing the ECSC, the EEC and Euratom, to be merged in the sixties by the Merger Treaty.[18] To establish an organization to supervise the observance of the rules laid down by the ratifying parties in a treaty is nothing special in itself. Neither is the establishment of an organization with the objective of realizing some coherence and co-operation between different nations, either worldwide or regional, anything new. The ILO and the United Nations may be regarded as typical examples of such organizations. On the European level, the Council of Europe fulfils such a role.

The difference between these organizations and the Comunity is to be found in the powers the Treaty has conferred on the Community institutions. The Commission, the Council of Ministers, the European Parliament and the Court of Justice together acquired a much more powerful position with regard to the member states than any other international organization.[19]

Within this institutional structure the federal nature of the four institutions differs. The Commission is a typically federal institution. It acts independently of the member states and its members cannot be considered representatives of the governments by whom they are appointed. The same goes for the European Parliament, which is directly elected by the citizens of the member states. The Court of Justice with its exclusive power to interpret Community law also has a federal character.

On the other hand, the Council of Ministers is a typically intergovernmental institution. This is important because the Council has the final power to decide on Community legislation. Nevertheless, it is significant how many powers are attributed to the federal institutions within the institutional structure.

For example, the Commission is entrusted with the negotiations concerning Treaties with third countries, if the issues concerned fall within the jurisdiction of the Community. Also, the Community institutions have, for example, a legislative power which does not differ that much from the legislative power of the member states.

More significantly, this legislative power is only partly exercised by the Council. The right of initiative resides with a typically federal institution, the Commission, which is obliged by the Treaty to act independently of the member states.

This is a federal element which should not be underestimated. The right of initiative, including the exclusive power to draft a first proposal, provides the Commission with the power to decide in which direction a proposal is going to head. Besides outright rejection, the only thing which remains for the member states is to amend the proposal during negotiations. Since amendments seldom completely change the original direction of a proposal, the right of initiative provides the Commission with an awesome power.[20]

The Commission and Council together adopt secondary legislation, which binds not only the member states, but also the subjects of those member states. Though the Council represents the member states and thus adds an intergovernmental element, this does not diminish the federal impact of this legislative power, because decisions in the Council can be achieved by a qualified majority.

While the possibility of binding member states against their will has been part of the Treaty since the beginning, the actual use of the procedure of majority decision making has been delayed for several decades. As has already been said, in the sixties, when the first steps to majority decisionmaking were taken, France strongly protested and even left its seat in the Council for half a year. As a result of the French action voting by majority was subsequently suspended for some twenty years.[21]

The Single European Act aimed to reinstate voting by majority,[22] which had been ignored for so long by the member states. The Community as well as the member states felt it was necessary to introduce majority voting. The reasons were to be found in the growth of the Community (by then ten members and more to come) and in the necessity of speeding up the decisionmaking process which by the early eighties had become very slow. Member states as well as European industry were clamouring for an acceleration of the integration process.[23]

The Single European Act achieved this result, but not without concessions to the member states. First, simple majority-voting procedures were altered in favour of qualified majority-voting procedures for those issues considered too important to be decided by only half of the member states. Second, and more important, the introduction of a qualified majority-voting procedure on internal market issues[24] contained an 'opting out' clause for member states. This 'opting out' clause provides member states with the option to apply their existing stricter standards in certain circumstances after the matter concerned is harmonized by a Community measure. Member states are allowed to apply the 'opting out' clause even when their stricter standards eventually hinder the completion of the internal market. The option to use the 'opting out' clause in this way is, however, very restricted.[25] It can only be used if the Commission accepts and confirms the necessity of applying the stricter standards. Nevertheless, the adoption of the 'opting out' clause was considered a major setback for the completion of the internal market.[26]

In the negotiations concerning the Treaty of Maastricht even more 'opting-out' clauses had to be accepted to achieve any result at all. The United Kingdom did not adopt the social chapter and reserved for itself the right to opt out of the European Monetary Union. Denmark would only accepted the monetary part of the Treaty if it were allowed to postpone its final decision until a referendum has been held.[27]

Nevertheless, the possibility of taking decisions by (qualified) majority-vote has been opened again and is being used. Already this has led to a renewed interest of the member states in the limitations of the regulatory powers of the Community. This topic will be discussed in chapter two.

While the fact that decisions can be taken by qualified majority-vote may be seen as a major federal element in the Treaty, this is not true for the way the legislative process is controlled by a parliament on a European level.[28]

Until recently the European Parliament had no decisive influence on Community legislation at all.[29] This has changed since the Treaty of Maastricht entered into force, but only for some policy areas. This so-called 'democratic deficit' existed for more than thirty years. Since the seventies, several efforts have been made to revise this undemocratic structure of the Community, but until recently none succeeded.[30]

In the original Treaty the European Parliament had only an advisory role. Though ignoring this role of the Parliament, in case the Treaty required it to give advice in the course of the decision-making process, might lead to an annulment of the decision,[31] it has never been very clear what, if any, influence these parliamentary opinions exercised.

The Single European Act introduced a (quite complicated) co-operation procedure which provided the Parliament with a greater ability to influence the legislative process. This included a right to amend proposals and a right to reject proposed legislation. If the Council wanted to ignore the parliamentary amendments or adopt a proposal against the wish of the Parliament, it had to decide to do so unanimously.[32] Nevertheless, the Parliament still had no decisive influence.

To some extent this has changed with the adoption of the Treaty of

Maastricht. On several issues this Treaty provides for a co-decision procedure in which the Parliament can reject and amend Commission proposals.[33] In such a case the Council is not empowered to overrule the Parliament. This co-decision procedure (which is very complicated in itself) does not apply to all Community decisions; however, the fact that it applies to decisions concerning the completion of the internal market is hugely important in itself. Limited as the co-decision procedure may be, it must be appreciated as a major step forward to a more democratic Community legislative process.

Another federal element in the Treaty is the role assigned to the Court of Justice. The Court has been exclusively entrusted with the interpretation of Treaty provisions and secondary legislation. This is particularly significant, because this interpretation may (through preliminary questions) be offered within national proceedings, so that Community subjects may immediately benefit from the applicable Treaty provisions and Community laws. In this respect the Court may be regarded as a constitutional court, though its role is more limited than the role assigned to its counterparts in the United States or Germany. The Court has exercised its power to interpret Community law in quite spectacular ways over the years. This will also be seen below.

Besides its role as constitutional court charged with the exclusive interpretation of Community law in the member states, the Court also acts as an administrative court for the Community itself. It is empowered to examine the lawfulness of the acts and decisions of Community institutions and it hears actions concerning the non-contractual liability of the Community.

The Court has taken this role quite seriously. It has never hesitated to annul the decisions of Community Institutions, if it considered these to be contrary to the Treaty provisions.

Even more significant is the way the Court extended the scope of the Treaty to incorporate general principles of justice in Community law.[34] This may best be illustrated through the Court's incorporation of human rights in Community law.[35] Though fundamental human rights do not form part of the Treaty, since the early seventies[36] the Court has consistently held that fundamental human rights must be regarded as an integral part of the general principles of law in Community law.[37] The Court went as far as virtually applying the European Convention on Human Rights, even though the Community is not a party to that convention.[38]

The structure of the Community itself can at least partly justify the characterization of the Treaty as a federal constitution. The Treaty provides for far-reaching legislative powers of the Community institutions without unanimous consent of the member states, and it enables the

Community judiciary to fulfill and extend its role as a constitutional court. While giving some leeway to the specific hang-ups of the member states, the recent modifications of the Treaty contained in the Treaty of Maastricht, do not alter that conclusion. These modifications may in the end prove to be a step forward.

2.2 *The Community legal order*

2.2.1 Treaty provisions and secondary law directly addressing individuals. Typical features of the Treaty which are seldom found in other treaties are the provisions directly addressing individuals. The most important provisions to be mentioned are the Treaty provisions on competition. Articles 85 and 86 of the Treaty directly confer obligations on private enterprises and these enterprises have to comply with the Treaty.

While most of the enforcement of Community law, through the requirement of implementation in national law, has been delegated to the member states, no state legislation is required to enforce compliance with the competition articles.[39] The enforcement is exclusively a Community affair. The Commission has the power to annul agreements between enterprises and to punish non-compliance. In addition, only the Commission has the power to grant enterprises exemptions from the effects of these provisions.

In essence articles 85 and 86 prohibit agreements between or behaviour of enterprises or groups of enterprises which restrict competition, thereby having an adverse effect on inter-state trade. If an agreement or behaviour meets those two criteria, the national competition law of the member state in which the enterprise operates is no longer relevant, even if it allows more than Community law. Conversely, if agreements or behaviour are violating national competition law but the Commission considers them to be in conformity with Community law, the national prohibitions are not relevant.

These far-reaching federal effects of articles 85 and 86 have never stopped the Court of Justice from interpreting them extensively. Although one might have expected some restraint, because Community law rarely concerned private enterprises in the beginning, this has not been the case. In competition law the Court behaves like any other national court would have done.[40] For example, it did not hesitate to extend the scope of article 86 (which contains only a prohibition of abuse of power on the market) to an attempt to achieve this position of power.[41]

The legal protection of individuals against acts of the Community addressing them is enshrined in the Treaty itself. This means that enterprises can appeal against decisions of the Commission based on the competition provisions and addressed to them. Article 173 provides individuals with a right of appeal to the Court against decisions of the Commission, which address them or affect them directly and individually.[42] The mirror image of article 173 is to be found in article 175, providing for a right of appeal against a failure to act by the Commission.

For a long period of time the articles concerning competition law were the only articles of the Treaty specifically directed towards individuals. This is not the case anymore, because the adoption of the Single European Act brought a new development in other areas. Since 1987 the Treaty has contained another article not directed towards the member states but towards private organizations. Article 118B explicitly provides for implementation of Community policy through collective agreements drawn up by private organizations.[43] The difference between article 118B and the articles on competition is, however, the obligatory nature of articles 85 and 86 EEC. Article 118B does not contain any obligation whatsoever for private organizations.

Nevertheless, an article like article 118B is quite a novelty in a treaty. The explicit recognition of organizations regulating the industrial relations area instead of the state, and the fact that these organizations are addressed in a Treaty primarily concerned with the member states can be seen as a federal and constitutional feature of the Treaty itself.

Article 118B addresses private organizations and is directed in particular towards the European Trade Unions Confederation (ETUC) and the federation of employers (UNICE). It provides for the option of implementing a social policy through collective agreements between those organizations. It contains an obligation for the Commission to stimulate the so-called social dialogue between the ETUC and the UNICE. The social dialogue is the European forum in which an embryonic form of collective bargaining takes place.[44] If the bargaining partners so desire, the social dialogue may lead to contractual relations on a supranational level. As late as 1988, however, the Commission did not view this option as realistic.[45]

The social dialogue has resulted in joint declarations of the partners on the introduction of new technologies[46] and worker participation.[47] However, these declarations have no binding character and should not be regarded as somehow implementing the Treaty, but rather as a form of soft law. Though soft law as such is not entirely without legal consequences under Community law,[48] it does not have the same effects as a collective agreement in national law. Soft law does not intend to create rights and obligations which can be enforced in court; collective agreements in most countries do.[49]

Community-wide legally binding measures, promulgated by private organizations, are difficult to achieve since on a Community level neither a legal framework for bargaining, nor mechanisms to solve legal disputes exist. Though ideas on this subject have been submitted, article 118B has never been backed up by secondary community law providing for such a legal framework.[50]

Though article 118B never led to the desired result, apparently eleven of the twelve member states deemed the option to regulate through collective agreements on the European level important enough to reinforce it in the Treaty of Maastricht. The Social Agreement added by Protocol[51] to the Treaty of Maastricht expands on the possibility of binding measures between management and trade unions (labour as it is called in the Agreement) to implement the Treaty. Article 4(2) of the Agreement gives the bargaining partners a choice as to which national legal systems to apply to the collective agreement once concluded, and it provides for the explicit option of implementing social policy through collective agreements. Since no such agreement has yet been concluded, it is not very clear what impact this extension of article 118B will have.

Besides those Treaty-provisions addressing individuals, the Treaty provides for secondary legal devices to bind individuals. There are two types of secondary law: directives and regulations. Both are to be found in article 189 of the Treaty, which is the basis of the legal devices used in Community law. The regulatory device directly addressing individuals is the regulation. According to article 189, regulations are generally applicable, binding in all respects and directly applicable in each member state. In other words: regulations do not differ from national statutory law.

Member states are not allowed to transform the contents of regulations in national legal provisions, unless the regulation itself explicitly allows them to do so.[52] This prohibition of transformation is logical. Regulations are laws in all respects, they can simply do without transformation. Besides, transformation in itself might lead to misinterpretations of the contents of regulations by the transforming authorities.

The Court has repeatedly held transformation to be incompatible with Community law on the grounds that the national provisions transforming a regulation might create an obstacle to the direct effect of the regulation and because it would conceal the origin of the the legal rule provided for by the regulation.[53] Such a concealment could tempt national judges, unaware of the origin of the rule, to interpret the regulation by themselves, without asking the Court of Justice preliminary questions.

Member states are not allowed to adopt measures which modify the scope of regulations, nor are they allowed to provide for additional requirements.[54] Additionally, they have lost the power to issue national measures in the area covered by the regulation, except where authorized by the Community rules itself.

Generally, regulations are to be applied and enforced by the competent authorities of the member states.[55] Which authority is competent to apply the regulation is to be determined by the member states. The Community is not empowered to do so.

The application of regulations, for example by granting licences provided for in the regulation, must be done in accordance with the regulation itself. Nevertheless, the national administrative requirements concerning individual decisions must necessarily be applied too, because Community law does not yet provide for the general rules of administrative law needed to process the applications for those decisions smoothly, and to provide for the necessary legal protection. This may lead to different practices in different member states, due to the differences between the administrative laws of the member states. The national administrative law, however, may not prevent the regulation from having its desired effect.

Since the Community also lacks the power to provide for (punitive) sanctions, the member states also have to take the necessary measures to apply and enforce the law. Only while acting in the framework of agricultural policy is the Community empowered to impose certain administrative sanctions.[56]

In most cases a regulation contains a provision requiring the member states to take the necessary measures to implement it. These provisions can be considered as a delegation of regulatory powers, a subject which will be discussed extensively in Chapter II.

In relation to the Community, member states, while applying regulations, must be regarded as analogous to local authorities, such as counties or municipalities. The case-law concerning this application in many ways resembles national case-law concerning national laws applied by local authorities.

The Treaty does not directly provide for the legal protection of individuals against illegal regulations. Nevertheless individuals can always base their claim on the illegality of a regulation in direct proceedings before the Court (in cases where a Community decision is based on a regulation) as well as within national proceedings.[57]

Article 184 of the Treaty explicitly recognizes this possibility, albeit for regulations only. In the author's opinion the explicit incorporation of this principle is not exactly necessary, since the Treaty already explicitly provides the Court with the power to examine the validity of secondary laws if member states, Community institutions, or individuals so demand.[58] This being so, it would be inconsistent and contrary to the principle of legal security if individuals could not invoke the illegality of a law on which an individual decision is based.[59] In Community law, illegal laws cannot impose obligations on indiviuals.[60] According to the Court, article 184 covers all acts of Community Institutions, whether in the form of a regulation or not.[61] If the act produces effects similar to a regulation, its illegality may be invoked.

If the illegality of an act is invoked within national proceedings, the national judge has no jurisdiction to decide on the validity of the disputed act. In such a case, the national judge is obliged to refer a preliminary question to the Court.[62]

The directly obligatory nature of articles 85 and 86 of the Treaty are unusual for international Treaties. The very fact that the whole field of competition is regulated by and enforced by the Community itself may be regarded as a typical federal feature of Community law. The same goes for the device of the regulation. Member states are required to apply and enforce regulations, but while doing this, their role is no different from the role of regional or local authorities in national constitutions and national law.

2.2.2 Direct applicability and supremacy of Treaty provisions not directed towards individuals. Perhaps the strongest federal feature of all in Community law is the concept of the direct applicability of Treaty provisions which were originally meant to be implemented by the member states. This concept was developed by the Court in the seventies.

When the Treaty entered into force in the fifties it was assumed that the duty to comply with its obligations would fall mainly on the member states. The Treaty transfers powers from the member states to the EC. It also contains obligations for the member states to establish a common market without borders between the member states. The member states are required to take the necessary measures to abolish discriminatory provisions in their legislation and to provide subjects of other member states with equal rights similar to the rights of their own nationals. Thus, on the face of it, most of the Treaty had a traditional structure which did not lead anyone to suspect that it would directly affect individuals.

However, as early as 1963, the Court of Justice held that Treaty provisions could be self-executing.[63] The Court ruled that the Community constituted a new legal order for the benefit of which the States had limited their own sovereign rights within limited fields. According to the Court, this new legal order counted among its subjects not only the member states but also the subjects of these member states.

The second important judgment in this respect was handed down in

1964. In the case of Costa-ENEL the Court ruled that Community law should prevail when national provisions are contrary to Community law.[64] This judgment was especially important for those areas in which domestic law differs radically from Community law. If Community law can be considered applicable, domestic law cannot be applied anymore.[65] An effect of this prevailing character of Community law, also called supremacy of Community law, which was not noted until many years later, is that national law should be interpreted in such a way as to be in compliance with the Community provision or secondary law concerned.[66] National judges are obliged to do so, even when the national legislator may have intended an entirely different interpretation of the national law concerned.

In 1974 the Court of Justice accepted the direct applicability of Treaty provisions in cases between individuals.[67]. In Walrave-Koch,[68] a judgment concerning the internal rules of a sports organization, it ruled that collective agreements and similar private collective arrangements should be in agreement with articles 48 and 59 of the Treaty, which provide for the free movement of workers and the freedom to provide services within the Community. In cases between individuals, the direct applicability of Treaty provisions concerning the free movement of services was established a few years later.[69]

In 1976 the Court completed this development. When Gabrielle Defrenne, the Belgian stewardess who, since she has three judgments to her name, can be characterized as the Joan of Arc of equal treatment law, claimed equal remuneration to her male colleagues as prescribed in article 119 of the Treaty, her employer responded that she could not rely on article 119, because this article addresses only member states and does not directly impose obligations on individuals. Taking the article literally, the employer was right. Article 119 clearly does not address private employers. The Court would have none of it, however. It ruled, as in earlier cases concerning free movement, that private companies were obliged to comply with article 119 (equal remuneration for men and women).[70]

These obligations for individuals inferred from the Treaty did not, however, absolve the member states from the duty to implement the Treaty provisions in their national law.

While the direct applicability of Treaty provisions imposing obligations on member states may have shocked the member states, the Court suprised them even more with its judgments on directives. Directives are the other legal device mentioned in article 189 which can be used to issue Community legislation. Directives explicitly address member states, and they are only binding as to the result to be achieved, so they definitely require transformation and implementation before they can achieve their binding effect. Nevertheless, in 1974, the Court of Justice ruled that in specific circumstances directives may be self-executing.[71] It held that directive provisions which contain clear enough obligations, are unconditional, and do not leave the member state any discretion while transforming the provision in national law, can be relied upon directly by individuals in national proceedings against the government.

In this author's opinion, these provisions can be relied upon only by those individuals with a specific interest in the actual adherence of member states to the provisions concerned. This element, however, has never been mentioned by the Court as a condition for direct effect of directive provisions. The question of whether individuals may rely on directive provisions which do not affect them specifically is not a theoretical one. A case in which an individual invoked provisions of a notification directive,[72] (a directive solely containing procedural requirements for the member states) is now pending before the Court.[73] In the author's opinion it is not very likely that the Court will rule that individuals can rely on directive provisions without regarding the question of whether the provision concerned affects the interests of the individual concerned.

The Court of Justice has held that directives can only confer obligations onto states. Obligations cannot be imposed on individuals or private organizations.[74] This leaves the question of which institutions related to or financed by the state, or acting on the state's behalf, must be regarded as included in 'the state' as far as the implementation of directives is concerned. This topic will be discussed extensively in chapter IV.

So the directly applicable provisions can only be relied on by individuals against the state, not against other individuals. However, if a member state has been negligent in implementing a directive, it has to apply the directly applicable provisions of the directive in all the capacities a state may assume. So whether a state acts in its public role as government, or in its private role as, for example, employer, its acts must comply with the directive concerned.[75]

Some authors by now advocate the direct applicability of directives between individuals: the so-called horizontal direct effect.[76] They feel the limited direct effect jeopardizes the full effect of Community law, and is no longer justifiable.

From a constitutional point of view, the present author, however, feels there still are objections against direct horizontal effect of directives.[77] The first objection is that the difference between directives and regulations would disappear. If directives confer obligations not only on member states but on individuals as well, in principle there is no longer any difference between directives and regulations. This is even more so since directives are often as detailed as regulations.

Another problem would be that member states would lose the opportunity to conduct their own policy while implementing the directive. Until now member states could conduct their own policy within the limits of the provisions of the directive. This leaves the member states some room for national policy,[78] especially when directive provisions are meant to provide for minimum requirements.[79] If directives address the member states as well as individuals, it would no longer be acceptable to interpret directive provisions as anything other than standard provisions. If directives impose obligations on the individual, the individual would be required to act in compliance with the directive provisions. At the same time, directives should, however, be transformed into national law, and the individual would also be required to act in compliance with that national law. Thus, if national law provides for something else, the individual might be compelled to act in compliance with two different statutory obligations which affect him or her directly at the same time.

In its recent judgment in the Dori case[80] the Court reaffirmed its position on the issue of horizontal direct effect. It argued that accepting direct effect of directives between individuals would provide the Community with a new power to issue rules directly conferring obligations on individuals, a power which is not provided by the Treaty itself.

The doctrines of direct effect and supremacy have led to some dispute about the validity of national law, which should not be applied because it is violating a directly applicable provision of Community law. Ter Kuile repeatedly advocated the view that such a national law or provision should be considered not only inapplicable, but invalid.[81] The difference between those two concepts is quite important in national law. If a law is inapplicable, it means the national government is not allowed to apply it to its subjects and will have to change or withdraw it. If a law is invalid, it means that it has never existed. No action whatsoever is needed to change it and one can even defend the view that the law it replaced is still the valid law to apply.

The Commission seems to share this view. It announced that national legislation on technical requirements for goods, which was adopted while violating a Community Directive on notification of such legislation, cannot be valid and therefore should not be applied. Because of the invalidity of this national law, the national law which it replaced was regarded as remaining in force.[82]

Ter Kuile bases his view on the judgments in the cases of Costa vs Enel[83] and Simmenthal.[84] In this last judgment the issue of validity of a national law which violated Community law was at stake.

In Simmenthal, the Court ruled that the entry into force of Community provisions which are directly effective does not only render any conflicting law inapplicable, but precludes the valid adoption of new legislation to the extent to which the latter would be incompatible with Community provisions.

The confusion surrounding this judgment stems from the words 'valid adoption'. While it is resoundingly clear that a new law violating Community law cannot be applied if it is incompatible with horizontal effective Treaty provisions or regulations, this might be different if the Community law concerned is a directive. While directives, as we have seen above, cannot directly impose obligations on individuals, a new law may have to be applied in favour of the individual if it imposes different (and specifically less interfering) obligations than the directive with which it is incompatible.

This means that from a Community point of view a national law cannot be considered formally invalid if it is incompatible with a directive. From a national point of view, the law is as valid as any other. The mere fact that it contradicts with a Community directive does not affect its validity whatsoever. But the Treaty itself does not distinguish between the effects of directives and regulations and horizontally directly effective Treaty provisions. The Treaty, in fact, does not provide for any rules concerning the formal status of national laws incompatible with Community legislation. Thus, since one cannot accept the formal invalidity of national laws incompatible with directives, there should be no reason to view a new law as formally invalid if it is incompatible with a horizontally direct effective Treaty provision or a regulation. Of course one has to admit that, if a new law is incompatible with a regulation or a horizontally direct effective Treaty provision, the fact that the national law cannot be applied under any circumstance renders it substantially invalid. Even when the national law is violating a directive, its inapplicability under all circumstances could render it substantially invalid. The formal validity as such, however, is not affected.

Other factors also point to the formal validity of national laws violating Community law. The Treaty, as we have seen above, only provides the Court with jurisdiction regarding the interpretation and validity of Community law. As the Court itself consistently held in preliminary procedures, it cannot interpret national law or judge its compatibility with Community law.[85]

The jurisdiction of the Court is limited to the question of whether the Community provisions should be applied instead of the national law. This limit to the jurisdiction of the Court leaves the question of whether a national law or provision which is incompatible with Community law is formally invalid to the national constitution. If in the national legal order judges are empowered to declare laws null and void because of incompatibility with laws of a higher legal order, they should do so in cases of incompatibility with Community law. If judges are not empowered to do so, it is up to the legislator to withdraw the incompatible law.

Until now national courts such as the Dutch Economic Appeals Court have held that a Community directive does not effectively render a national law invalid.[86] The case concerned dealt with a national law violating the Notification Directive on which the Commission had issued its convocation.[87] In a comparable case on another directive containing procedural requirements, the Court of Justice maintained the same point of view with regard to the effects of the directive on the national law.[88] A case concerning the specific question of national laws violating a Community directive is pending before the Court.[89]

Ter Kuile, however, goes even further where the validity of national laws which are incompatible with Community law is concerned. He also maintains the view that the direct applicability and supremacy of Community law have as their consequence the fact that judgments of the highest national judge which violate Community law cannot be effective between the parties.[90] He derives this conclusion partly from the abovementioned case-law and from the obligation for the highest judge to ask preliminary questions to the Court, if there is any doubt about the interpretation of Community law. According to Ter Kuile, even the execution of a judgment by the winner of such a case may be illegal.

He assumes this non-effective nature could only be achieved after a second judgment concerning an analogous case, in which the Court of Justice would substantially rule the first judgment incompatible with Community law. To accept this view might mean that every judgment of the highest national Court would be provisional if it contains an element of Community law and the national judge did not consider it necessary to ask preliminary questions.

Though the author agrees with Ter Kuile that such an incompatible judgment would be a violation of Community law by the member state as a whole[91] for which that member state can be held liable,[92] she does not agree with his assumption that the judgment concerned would be without any effect between the parties. Again, the Community does not have any jurisdiction regarding the binding effect of national judgments. The binding effect of those judgments is purely a matter of national law. That individuals have no direct appeal to the Court of Justice in procedures concerning the compatibility of domestic law with Community law points to the fact that member states, while concluding the Treaty, did not wish to entrust the Court of Justice with jurisdiction in these matters.

To assume that this jurisdiction is derived from judgments concerning the applicability of Community law is going way beyond the scope of these judgments.

3 The political growth towards a federal Community: the Treaty of Maastricht

While the legal order of the Community has contained some of the elements of a federal state since the fifties,[93] as we saw above the Treaties establishing the European Community still does not include all the necessary elements to make it a federal constitution. The Treaty still lacks certain elements which would make the Community a federal state. The lack of the power to represent the Community in all external affairs and the lack of a Community defence policy can be counted among those omissions. Also, the scope of the Treaty itself has long been considered to be too limited for it to constitute a federal state.

Originally the scope of the Treaty was economic only; the EC was meant to be an economic organization. Even the incorporation of social provisions in the Treaty, such as article 119 (equal remuneration of men and women), were economically inspired.[94] This economic spirit has not been altered by later revisions of the Treaty and has certainly been strengthened by the intended growth to a Monetary Union with a European Central Bank and a single European currency as provided for in the Treaty of Maastricht.[95]

Nevertheless, by now to characterize the Treaty as a purely economic treaty would be a denial of the developments which have taken place since the fifties. The Community by now encompasses much more than just an economic organization. This change has been caused by more than one factor.

Firstly, the scope of the Treaty itself allowed the Community to develop into a more widely operating organization. This scope has been ill-defined from the beginning. In fact the adjective 'economic' in itself does not define anything. It implicitly includes every activity which already is, or has the potential of being, commercially exploited. Since there are not that many activities which are definitely not capable of commercial exploitation, the scope of the Treaty implicitly includes a range of policies originally not intended to be regulated by the Community.

A recent example is the discussion concerning the availibility of the technique of *in vitro* fertilization for women beyond menopause. Since *in vitro* fertilization is a medical service, and medical services are services under article 59 of the Treaty,[96] a single member state cannot preclude women beyond menopause to be provided with this service, simply by prohibiting *in vitro* fertilization beyond a certain age in its national law. The women concerned can easily travel to a member state with less restrictive laws to avail themselves of this service.

So the country most in favour of such a prohibition, i.e. France, immediately started a plea for Community legislation on this subject.[97] France thereby ignored the fact that the question of whether it is desirable or not that women beyond menopause would be able to bear children following treatment in *in vitro* fertilization centres, is much more an ethical then an economic one. By clamouring for Community legislation, France implicitly acknowledged Community jurisdiction on this very non-economic issue. This process of implicit inclusion of basically non-economic policies in the scope of the Treaty will be discussed extensively in Chapter II.

Secondly, because of the addition of issues unexpectedly falling within the scope of the Treaty, member states have developed the tendency to include complete policy areas in Community policymaking. Though many of these policy areas were never originally intended to be the object of Community influence, member states, industry, and individuals considered the addition a necessity for reasons of fair competition between the different member states or as protection against acitivities in other member states. So they clamoured for Community action on policy areas not very closely related to the original economic Treaty.

An example of this last development is the addition of the environmental paragraph through the Single European Act in 1987. Since some member states started with national measures to protect the environment, Community-wide environmental legislation was deemed necessary to balance the economic freedoms provided for by the Treaty. Without Community legislation on this matter, the member state with the least restrictive legislation might profit from the higher standards in other member states, while at the same time undermining those standards. Thus the member state with the most developed environmental policy might be at a disadvantage in the interstate competition.

However, no specific power to regulate on environmental matters existed in the Treaty. Nevertheless, environmental measures were actually promulgated during the seventies and eighties.[98] The legal basis used was article 235, which within the framework of the common market provides for powers to take the necessary measures, even if the Community does not provide for any specific power to regulate.

In 1987, the existing power of the Community to regulate was considered too restrictive, so a separate paragraph on environmental policy was inserted in the Treaty. Since then the Community has been provided with specific powers to regulate and conduct a policy on this subject.[99]

This development of the inclusion of new policy fields in the Treaty was continued in the Treaty of Maastricht. This Treaty added another six policy fields to the Community jurisdiction: education, vocational training, health, culture, youth and consumer protection. Unlike the incorporation of the environmental paragraph, the incorporation of these policy fields was primarily meant to limit the influence that the Community exercises in these policy areas through the provisions concerning the internal market.[100] Since the internal market, according to the case-law of the Court, includes every kind of economic activity, it also applies to activities which fall within the scope of these policy areas. The inclusion of the new paragraphs incorporated in the Treaty is meant to determine the division of powers between the member states and the Community in those policy areas.

The education and vocational training paragraphs confer the power to contribute to the quality of education by encouraging co-operation between member states to the Community. It does not transfer any regulatory powers from the member states to the Community.

In the field of culture the Community is empowered to contribute to the flowering of the cultures of the member states, while respecting their national and regional diversity and at the same time bringing the common cultural heritage to the fore. The health paragraph empowers the Community to contribute to ensuring of a high level of human health protection. This contribution has to be made through encouraging co-operation between the member states and if necessary through the lending of support to the member states. The Community aim should be the encouragement of health information and education, and the prevention of diseases, in particular the major health scourges, including drug addiction.

In all of these fields the power to harmonize the laws or regulations of the member states is explicitly excluded. The only power conferred is the power to take incentive measures. In this respect the powers of the Community are restricted. Because of this restriction the meaning of the addition of the new policy areas to the jurisdiction of the Community is not yet clear.

Though the aim of including these policy areas may have been to protect member states against Community influence, inclusion in the Treaty is always a two-edged sword. However restricted, the inclusion implies that the Community definitely has a task here. Member states simply cannot argue anymore that these fields belong exclusively to their own jurisdiction; they provided the Community with powers to act, however limited these powers may be. Most certainly, the addition of powers will eventually have its consequences. Before a balance between member states and Community is achieved, however, this limited addition of powers may create its own problems in the future.

It is because of this that since the adoption of the Treaty of Maastricht it is hardly possible anymore to characterize the Community as a classic international organization with only a limited (i.e. economic) scope. By now the Treaty encompasses quite a few policy areas which are definitely not economic. The mere fact that the powers of the Community to regulate these policy areas are limited does not affect this conclusion. This means that, though the Treaty of Maastricht does not change the power stucture as such that much, the incorporation of these typically national and non-economic policy areas in the Treaty strengthens the federal character of the Community.

While extending the scope of the Treaty beyond its original economic content, and thereby sowing new seeds for a political growth to a federal level, the Treaty of Maastricht at the same time strengthens the intergovernmental approach of the European Union as a whole. The European political co-operation on a common foreign and security policy, the principles of which were already incorporated in the Single European Act, has been extended in the Treaty of Maastricht, but it has not been provided with the supranational instruments which the original Community has. Co-operation in the spheres of justice and home affairs also has been kept out of the Community structure. Although these policy areas have been incorporated in the Maastricht Treaty, this has been done on a purely intergovernmental basis. The co-operation on these last matters is intended to deal with issues such as asylum seekers and the fight against international crime.

So the Treaty of Maastricht in fact provides for a European Union based on three pillars. Firstly, there is the already existing European Community now embracing much more than economics. Secondly there is the existing but extended European political co-operation dealing with external affairs, and thirdly there is the newly found co-operation on certain internal affairs. Two of those three pillars have an entirely intergovernmental character.

This addition and strengthening of the intergovernmental elements in the co-operation between the member states can be approached in two different ways. One may say that the federal character of the organization as a whole is weakened. The supranational part of the Treaty can be viewed as just one of three integral parts of the organizational structure. In this view the Community has reverted (at least partly) to the status of international organization.

On the other hand one may view the inclusion of these traditionally national policy areas, though in the form of co-operation, in a Treaty which also establishes a federal organization, as a first step to incorporate these areas in the supranational Community structure.[101] The mere fact that member states are obliged by the Treaty to co-operate on these issues within the Community atmosphere and in the presence of Community institutions such as the Commission, may eventually lead to an extension of the Community sphere of influence in these matters.

4 Concluding remarks

The voyage the six states and their seventh companion embarked upon in the fifties has already taken them to surprising destinations. Their numbers kept growing and along the way they encountered successes as well as disappointments and sometimes even outright failures. Sometimes they travelled fast, at other times they nearly halted. At times they were handicapped by differences of opinion between the travellers, some of whom were more reluctant than others. This sometimes led to small battles about the direction in which to go and sometimes to bigger battles about the eventual destination. While at times the fighting slowed them down, their voyage has not yet come to an end.

Though not yet old, the Community already has some history. When the Treaty establishing the EEC was adopted, probably only a few idealists expected the Community to develop into some kind of United States of Europe. A decade later even their expectations must have been lowered, since the Luxembourg crisis did not leave much room for federal ideals. Also, the stagnation in decision making in the seventies and the reputation of moneywasting the Community earned in those days make it rather surprising that the question of whether the Community will develop into a full-fledged federation is still relevant. Though the outcome cannot be predicted, apparently a federation is still among the possibilities.

This is not to say that the Community already is a federation, or that the member states desire it to be one. The negotiations to achieve the Treaty of Maastricht have been difficult enough and the outcome does not strengthen the federal elements in the Treaty in all respects. Though the extension of the powers of the European Parliament may be regarded as a development on the way to achieve a more federal organization, the addition of the two intergovernmental pillars to the Community structure can just as easily be seen as a setback. More important perhaps is that the development of the Community depends on more than legal or political factors alone. The way other European countries and especially the Eastern European countries develop may be an equally important factor.[102] The economic development of these last countries could, if lagging behind too far, seriously jeopardize economic growth in, and therefore the unity between the Community members.

Nevertheless, one may say that the history of the Community itself, especially with regard to the process of decision making, the transfer of powers, the enforcement of its legal order and the effects of Community law on national law, have already presented the member states with unforeseen (and sometimes unwanted) consequences. These consequences lead to the conclusion that in some respects the Treaty indeed resembles a constitution and may be treated that way by the member states and their citizens.

At the same time, the limitations on the powers of the Community as laid down in the Treaty provide for a very diffuse legal order which too often presents citizens (and lawyers) with incomprehensible legal niceties. These elements will be discussed in the next three chapters.

Notes

1. Treaty of 25 March 1957, entered into force 1 January 1958.
2. Pinder (1986), European Community and National State: a case for a neo-federalism, *International affairs*, 41-54.
3. In a speech delivered at the College of Europe in Bruges on 20 September 1988, the then Prime Minister of the United Kingdom, Margaret Thatcher, made clear she held this view. See also Kapteyn (1993), Markt zonder staat, Bussum.
4. Gorbey (1993), *Stilstand is vooruitgang. De dialectiek van het Europese integratieproces*, Van Gorkum en Comp, Assen.
5. This French position led to the agreement of Luxembourg of January 1966, through which the voting by majority on Community decisions was suspended until the early eighties.
6. OJ 1984, C 77 p. 33-52.
7. Bieber, Jaque, Weiler, (eds.) (1985), *An ever closer Union, A critical analysis of the Draft Treaty establishing the European Union*, European University Institute, Florence.
8. Treaty of 17 February 1986, OJ 1987 L 169, entered into force 1 July 1987.
9. De Zwaan (1986), The Single European Act, Conclusion of a Unique Document, *Common Market Law Review*, 747.
10. Treaty on a European Union, 7 February 1992, OJ 1992, C 191, entered into force 1 November 1993.
11. Bundesverfassungsgericht, 2 BvR 3124/92 en 2 BvR 2159/92, 12 October

1993 on the Treaty of Maastricht.

12. Inserted by the Treaty of Maastricht in the EC-Treaty (article 3B).
13. On the history of the EC-treaties, Kapteyn, VerLoren van Themaat, Gormley (1989), *Introduction to the Law of the European Communities*, Kluwer, Deventer, Chapter I.
14. For example article 18 of the Treaty of Vienna concerning the law of treaties, 23 May 1969; to be found in the Dutch Trb. 1977, 169.
15. Temple Lang (1990), Community Constitutional Law: Article 5 EEC Treaty, *27 Common Market Law Review,* 645 at 659-661.
16. Treaty of Paris, 18 April 1951; entered into force 23 July 1952.
17. Striking examples of this retreating behaviour of the member states are the inclusion in the Treaty of Maastricht of a protocol revising article 119 EC-treaty to limit the consequences of the Barber-judgment (case C-262/88, [1990] ECR 1889 on the application of the equal remuneration provision on occupational pensions) and the protocol on Ireland concerning the application of the constitutional protection of the unborn child.
18. Treaty of April 8, 1965; entered into force July 29, 1967; see Kapteyn, Verloren van Themaat, Gormley, *supra* at 33-34.
19. The only institution playing a similar role is the Security Council of the United Nations, which can also bind member states against their will. The scope of the powers of the Security Council is, however, much more limited.
20. There has been some criticism and anxiety about the fulfilling of the initiating role by the Commission especially since the establishment of the European Council, which specifically develops general policy-lines; see e.g. Kapteyn, VerLoren van Themaat, Gormley, *supra* at 108.
21. Kranz (1992), La vote dans la pratique du Conceil des Ministres des Communautés européennes, *Revue Trimestrielle de Droit Européen*, 104.
22. For the history of the Single Act, see Korte (1989), Institutionele implicaties van de Europese Akte; de Europese Akte en de instellingen van de EG, *Ars Aequi* 38(1989)5.
23. See for example the publication of Philips Eindhoven (1984), *Europe 1990, an agenda for action*, Eindhoven.
24. Article 100A, inserted by the Single European Act. The opting out clause is laid down in section four.
25. Kapteyn, VerLoren van Themaat, Gormley, *supra* at 475.
26. Pescatore (1987), Some critical remarks on the Single European Act, *Common Market Law Review* no. 1.
27. Steyger (1992), Eenwording door versnippering, de overeenkomst betreffende de Europese economische ruimte, *RegelMaat*, 1992-4, 94.
28. The only real controlling power the Parliament has is the control over the EC-budget. See e.g. Kapteyn, VerLoren van Themaat, Gormley, *supra* at 236-237, also Notenboom (1988), *Het Europees parlement en de financiën*, Staatsdrukkerij en Staatsuitgeverij (SDU), Den Haag.
29. The meagre role of the Parliament has led to the remarkable result that the Parliament is empowered to challenge the legality of Community legislation

before the Court, See e.g. case 70/88, [1990] ECR I-2041.

30. For example the Vedel-report, Bulletin EEC, suppl. 4/72, p. 42, the report of the Commission, Bulletin EEC, suppl. 5/75 and the Report Bertrand, EPW, 174/75.
31. Cases 138/79, Roquette, [1980] ECR 3333; 139/79, Maizena, [1980] ECR 3393.
32. Steyger (1990), Vertrouwen is goed, controle is beter; bevoegdheidsoverdracht en democratische controle in pre-federaal Europa, in Heringa, Verheij (eds.), *Publiekrechtelijke bewegingen*, Kluwer, Deventer, 117-137.
33. The new article 189B of the EC-Treaty, inserted by the Treaty of Maastricht.
34. De Witte (1991), Community Law and National Constitutional Values, *Legal issues of European Integration*, 1991/2, 1-2; also Temple Lang (1991), The Sphere in which Member States are obliged to comply with the General Principles of Law and Community Fundamental Rights Principles, *Legal Issues of European Integration*, 1991/2, 2335.
35. Rasmussen (1986), *On Law and Policy in the European Court of Justice*, Nijhoff Publishers, Dordrecht, 390-409.
36. Before 1969, the Court did not feel empowered to hear claims that human rights were violated, see the cases 1/58, Stork vs High Authority, [1959] ECR 17; joined cases 36-38 and 40/59, 'Präsident', 'Geitling', 'Mausegatt' and Nold vs High Authority, [1960] ECR 423; case 40/64, Sgarlata vs Commission, [1965] ECR 215.
37. Case 29/69, [1969] ECR 419, case 11/70, Internationale Handelsgesellschaft, [1970] ECR 1125; see for an overview Betten (1985), *The right to strike in Community Law*, North Holland, The Hague, 30-37.
38. Case 4/73, J. Nold vs Commission, [1974] ECR 491; see also case 136/79, National Panasonic, [1980] ECR 2033.
39. Which does not mean state-legislation in itself might not be regarded as non compliant with the articles 85 and 86, see e.g. cases 267/86, Van Eycke, [1988] ECR 4769; 311/85, Vlaamse reisbureau's, [1987] ECR 3801. See also Joliet (1988), Réglementation étatiques anti-concurrentielles et droit communautaire, *Cahiers de droit communautaire*, 363.
40. Rasmussen, *supra* at 136-137.
41. Case 6/72, Continental Can, [1973] ECR 215.
42. A wealth of case-law has developed over the years; for an overview see e.g. Kapteyn, VerLoren van Themaat, Gormley, *supra* at 290-297.
43. Steyger (1993), European Community Law and the self-regulatory Capacity of Society, *Journal of Common Market Studies*, Volume 31 no. 2 June, 174-175.
44. Steyger (1990), *Medezeggenschap bij veiligheid en gezondheid: de Europese regelingen*, Kluwer, Deventer, 60-61.
45. Commission of the European Communities (1988), *Social Europe, the social dimension of the internal market*, OOPEC, Luxembourg, 73.
46. Joint declaration of Val Duchesse, 12 November 1985.
47. Joint declaration of Val Duchesse, 6 March 1987.

48. Wellens, Borchardt (1989), Soft Law in European Community Law, *European Law Review*, 267-321 at 304-305.
49. Ganz (1987), *Quasi-legislation; Recent Developments in Secondary Legislation*, Sweet & Maxwell, London.
50. Jacobs (1986), *Het recht op collectief onderhandelen in rechtsvergelijkend en Europees perspectief*, Samsom/H.D. Tjeenk Willink, Alphen a/d Rijn, 400 and 419-425.
51. Since it was not feasible to extend the social policy in the negotiations concerning the Treaty on the European Political Union in Maastricht in December 1991 an Agreement of all member states except Great Britain has been concluded which aims to develop community social policy.
52. Wrongly in this respect the Dutch 'Aanwijzingen voor de regelgeving' (a code of practice on drafting legislation for the civil service). In this document (aanwijzing 340) it is stipulated that provisions of regulations may be transformed into national law, if non-transformation leads to incomprehensible national law. See T.C. Borman (ed.) (1993), *Aanwijzingen voor de regelgeving*, SDU Uitgeverij, Den Haag.
53. Cases 39/72, Commission vs Italy, [1973] ECR 101; 50/76, Amsterdam Bulb BV vs Produktschap voor Siergewassen, [1977] ECR 137; 94/77, Fratelli Zerbone vs Amministrazione delle Fianze della Stato, [1978] ECR 99.
54. Case 40/69, Hauptzollamt Hamburg-Oberelbe vs Fa. Bollmann, [1970] ECR 69; case 74/69, Hauptzollamt Bremen-Freihafen vs Waren-Import-Gesellschaft Krohn, [1970] ECR 451.
55. The exceptions being the Regulations concerning competition law.
56. On whether a sanction must be considered punitive see case C-240/92, Germany vs Commission, [1992] ECR nyr; German text also published in RegelMaat, 1993/1, 38.
57. An interesting case in this respect is case C-188/92, TWD Textilwerke Deggendorf vs Germany, pending, conclusion of A-G Jacobs of 15 September 1993.
58. This is not always the case; the Dutch Constitution explicitly prohibits the national judge to examine the constitutional validity of statutory laws adopted by Parliament (article 120 Grondwet).
59. Van Rijn (1978), *Exceptie van onwettigheid en prejudiciele procedure inzake geldigheid van gemeenschapsrecht*, Kluwer, Deventer, 172, 261.
60. Whether they can confer rights on individuals depends on the application of the principle of legal security.
61. Case 92/78, Simmenthal SpA vs Commission, [1979] ECR 777.
62. Case 314/85, Foto-Frost vs. Hauptzollamt Lübeck-Ost, [1987] ECR 4199.
63. Case 26/62, Van Gend en Loos vs Nederlandse administratie der belastingen, [1963] ECR 1.
64. Case 6/64, Costa vs ENEL, [1964] ECR 585.
65. Case 14/68, Wilhelm et. al vs Bundeskartellamt, [1969] ECR 1.
66. Case 51/76, VNO, [1977] ECR 113; case 38/77, ENKA, [1977] ECR 2203; case 80/86, Kolpinghuis, [1987] ECR 3969.

67. Already in 1971 the Court implicitly took the same stand (Case 78/70, Deutsche Gramofon Gesellschaft GmbH vs Metro-SB-Grossmarkte, [1971] ECR 487).
68. Case 36/74, Walrave and Koch vs Association Union Cycliste Internationale, [1974] ECR 1405.
69. Case 90/76, SRL Ufficio Henry van Ameyde vs SRL Ufficio Centrale Italiano, [1977] ECR 1091.
70. Case 43/75, Gabrielle Defrenne vs Sabena Airlines, [1976] ECR 455.
71. Case 41/74, Yvonne van Duyn vs Home Office, [1974] ECR 1337.
72. Dir. 83/189, OJ 1983 L 109.
73. Case C-194/94, SA C.I.A. Security International vs SA Signalson and SPRL Securitel, pending.
74. Case 152/84, Marshall, [1986] ECR 723; case 80/86, Kolpinghuis, [1987] ECR 3969.
75. Case 152/84, *supra*; see Steyger (1991), De directe toepassing van richtlijnen door anderen dan de Staat, *RegelMaat* no. 1, 11.
76. Prechal (1990), Remedies after Marshall, *Common Market Law Review*, Summer, see also the Conclusion of A-G van Gerven in case C-271/91, Marshall vs Southampton and South West Hampshire Area Health Authority II, [1993] ECR nyr.
77. Steyger (1993), JCMSt, *supra* at 184-185.
78. See also C-11/92, R. vs Secretary of State for Health, *ex parte* Gallagher and others, 22 June 1993 [1993], ECR nyr, in which a preliminary question is asked concerning minimum and standard requirements in Directive 89/622 concerning the labelling of tobacco products.
79. Timmermans (1980), Harmonisatie van wetgeving en Nederlands recht; beeld van bewogen beweging, *R.M. Themis*, 406-431.
80. Case C-91/92, Paola Faccini Dori vs Recreb Srl. 14 July 1994, [1994] ECR nyr.
81. Ter Kuile (1989), *Hoe ver ligt Den Haag nog van Brussel*, Kluwer, Deventer, Chapter II.
82. Convocation of the Commission 86/c245/05 OJ 1986, C 1\245.
83. Case 6/64, *supra*.
84. Case 106/77, Simmenthal, [1978] ECR 629.
85. Case 20/64, Albatros vs Sopeco, [1965] ECR 1.
86. CBB, 30 January 1991 no. 89/1357/90/195, AB 1992 no. 8
87. See note 79.
88. Case 380/87, Enichem Base c.s. vs Comune di Cinisello Balsamo, [1989] ECR 2491.
89. See case C-194/94, SA C.I.A. Security International vs SA Signalson SPRL Securitel, pending, in which the question of the direct effect of the notification directive is an explicit issue. See also the conclusion of A-G Van Gerven in joined cases C-52/93 and C-61/93, Commission vs the Netherlands, [1994] ECR nyr.
90. Ter Kuile (1993), Het verband tussen artikel 177 EC, aalscholvers en pursers, *Nederlands Juristenblad*, 1136-1141.

91. In the seventies, A-G Warner concluded that an error by a judge on Community law could not be regarded as a violation of Community law under article 169; conclusion in case 9/75, Meyer-Burckhardt, [1975] ECR 1171.
92. According to the Francovich judgment, cases C-6 and C-9/90, Francovich and Bonifaci, [1991] ECR I-5357.
93. Lasok, Stone (1987), *Conflict of Laws in the European Community*, Professional Books, Abingdon, 15-16.
94. Prechal, Burrows (1990), *Gender Discrimination Law of the European Community*, Dartmouth Publishing Company, Aldershot, 49.
95. Articles 105-109 EC-Treaty as amended by the Treaty of Maastricht. Denmark and Great Britain reserved the right to opt out of the so-called third stage of the monetary union. The German Constitutional Court maintains that the German Constitution reserves such an opting out possibility for Germany too (Bundesverfassungsgericht, 12 October 1993, 2 BvR 2134/92 en 2 BvR 2159/92).
96. Case 286/82, Luise & Carbone vs Ministero del Tesoro, [1984] ECR 377; case C-159/90, S.P.U,C. vs Grogan, [1991] ECR 4685.
97. See e.g. the article on this subject in *Vrij Nederland* of 14 January 1994.
98. One of the most far-reaching measures in this field is the Directive on the protection of Wild Birds, Dir. 79/409, OJ 1979, L 103.
99. Sevenster (1992), *Milieubeleid en gemeenschapsrecht*, Kluwer, Deventer.
100. See Chapter III.
101. Such a development can be seen explicitly in article K.9 of the Treaty of Maastricht which allows for the possibility of transferring several issues of the intergovernmental policy areas of Justice and Home Affairs to the jurisdiction of the Community; see section II.2.
102. A significant example may be that six of the seven (former) EFTA-states have joined the internal market by ratifying the Treaty on a European Economic Area (Treaty of Porto, 2 May 1992, doc. 5994/1/92 ref. 1 AELE 31, see also OOPEC Luxembourg, ISBN 92-826-3448-5).

II Grabbing for power

The distribution of powers in the Community

1 Introduction

The division of powers between the member states and the federation is one of the most important matters to be regulated in a federal constitution. Though the question whether the Treaty may be characterized as a federal constitution can, as we have seen, not be finally answered yet, it is clear that through adopting the Treaty the member states have transferred a part of their sovereignty to the Community.[1] Thus, even though the status of the Community is not clear, the problem of the division of powers does occur in the same way as in an acknowledged federation.

Usually a federation is established by already existing units (states or regions) with autonomous regulatory powers. In most cases a federation therefore derives its regulating power from those units. Thus the establishment of a federation requires the transfer of regulatory powers (and with that of sovereignty) from the members of the federation to the federation itself. This means the constitution has to provide the federation with the authority to regulate.

On the other hand, the members of a federation will have an established interest in restraining the federation from acquiring too much power.[2] Therefore, by its nature any federal constitution limits the transferred powers to a certain extent. All these elements are to be found in the Treaty.

Once a federal constitution is adopted, there is (usually) a federal court which ultimately interprets the constitution. Over the years, federal courts have tended to extend (and sometimes stretch) the powers of the federation in order to enable the federation to act effectively. The member states pay the price for these extensions in the form of an (often unintended) loss of power to the federation.[3] One can also see this happening in the Community.

This chapter will focus on the distribution of powers in the Community and the way these powers are transferred from the member states to the federation. Special attention will be paid to the case-law of the Court of Justice concerning the interpretation of the Treaty with respect to the jurisdiction of the Community and its consequences for the regulatory powers of the Community. Also, the limits of the Treaty and the consequences of those limits for the individual in particular will be discussed.

Finally, attention will be paid to the change that occurs in the relation between the Community and its member states, once the transfer of powers on an issue has been accomplished. After the transfer has been achieved, there may still be a need to delegate regulatory powers within the Community, either from one Community institution to another or from the Community to the member states. The power to delegate is necessary to enable the Community to implement Community laws.

Delegation of regulatory power creates its own legal problems such as what may be delegated and the boundaries of the discretionary powers to be delegated. In the Community, the question also arises as to who has the right to interpret the national provisions in case these provisions are adopted or used as a result of delegation by the Community. These questions are addressed in the third section of this chapter.

2 The transfer of powers to the Community

The distribution of powers between the Community and the member states is based on the doctrine of two separate legal orders which are related to each other in several ways; they are sometimes even intertwined, but nevertheless clearly distinct. As has already been said in section I.2.2.2., the transfer of a power to the Community only slightly affects the internal constitutional legal order of the member states. It does limit the powers of the member states to make decisions or policy at will on those areas directly falling within the scope of the Treaty or regulated by the Community. Additionally, it may require the alteration or withdrawal of existing legislation in the member states if this legislation violates Community law. However, the transfer of a power definitely does not lead to the invalidity of national laws even when these laws violate (directly applicable) Treaty provisions or secondary law.

Transfer of powers from the member states to the Community can be accomplished in various ways. Once a power is transferred, however, member states no longer have jurisdiction to act in that field except within the limits the Community sets for them. The transfer of powers to the Community is irreversible[4]. Already in 1971 the Court ruled that

> '...given that the Member States agreed to establish a Community of unlimited duration, having permanent institutions invested with real powers, stemming from a limitation of authority or transfer of powers from the States to that Community. .... (the powers)... thus conferred could not, therefore, be withdrawn from the Community, nor could the objectives with which such powers are concerned be restored to the field of authority of the Member States alone, except by virtue of an express provision of the Treaty'.[5]

Even if the Community fails to implement a Treaty provision and therefore is in default, it does not lose its power to act. In such a case, the member states are no longer allowed to act at will in the field concerned.[6] Nevertheless, in such a situation member states may be entitled to maintain or introduce national measures if their action can be regarded as necessary to achieve the objectives of the Treaty.[7] In such circumstances, these measures are not to be regarded as an exercise of the autonomous powers of the member state, but as being taken in compliance with the duty of co-operation imposed by article 5 of the Treaty in order to achieve the common objectives. The measures therefore have a temporary nature and should cease to be applied as soon as Community measures are introduced.[8]

The Community, unlike its member states, does not possess sovereign legislative power in the way legislative bodies in the member states do. In principle the Community has only those powers explicitly conferred by the three Treaties establishing the Community.[9] The scope of any power granted to the Community is limited by the Treaty provision which grants it. The Treaty provision may provide a legal basis to promulgate secondary legislation on a subject. In that case the power bestowed on the Community extends to all measures necessary to reach the objectives envisaged by the relevant article of the Treaty, within the limits of that article. For example, article 6 of the Treaty provides for a legal basis to adopt rules designed to prohibit discrimination. Since article 6 only prohibits discrimination on the grounds of nationality, rules designed to prohibit discrimination on other grounds (such as gender or race) cannot be promulgated on the basis of article 6.

Thus a subject can only be regulated by the Community if and when an appropriate legal basis can be found in the Treaty. If not, no power to legislate exists. Whether a given legal basis can be considered sufficient is to be decided in the first instance by the Community legislator, but in in case of disagreement, it is the Court which decides in the last resort. If a subject falls within the scope of two legal bases at once, the Community legislator, and ultimately the Court of Justice, must decide which legal basis is the most appropriate.[10] Since the different legal bases carry with them different voting procedures (e.g. qualified majority or unanimity), this decision is a highly political one. Over the years a substantial body of case-law has been developed concerning the choice of the appropriate legal basis.[11]

This simple concept of limited powers led to an extension of the powers of the Community not anticipated or envisaged when the Treaty was adopted in the 1950's. This extension followed from the scope of the different legal bases in the Treaty and the way these varying scopes were constructed by the Court of Justice.

Three kinds of legal bases can be distinguished. The first kind are those which enable the Community to issue legislation in a specific policy area such as article 43(2) on agricultural policy or article 130S on environmental policy.[12] The second kind are those legal bases empowering the Community to issue legislation on a specific subject such as the free movement of workers or the abolition of restrictions on the right of establishment.

Third, there are those legal bases which enable the Community to issue legislation to achieve the objectives of the Treaty, such as the establishment and the completion of the internal market.

The legal bases empowering the Community to regulate in specific policy areas are usually reasonably clear about the extent of the power they bestow on the Community.[13] These legal bases are already limited because of the substance of the policy area itself. For example, though opinions may differ on the exact scope of the concept of 'working environment and health and safety of workers' in article 118A of the Treaty, it is clear that directives based on this article, must be related in some way to working conditions. Legislation concerning, say, the environment, can definitely not be based on article 118A, however crucial a clean environment may be to the health and safety of all of us, including workers. The relationship is simply too indirect. Also, in most legal bases concerning specific policy areas, the restrictions on the powers of the Community are laid down explicitly.

The legal bases which empower the Community to regulate on specific parts of the internal market are also more or less clear about the powers they provide the Community with: the power to issue regulations or directives to harmonize the subjects concerned. For example, a legal basis providing the Community with the power to regulate the free movement of workers or the abolition of restrictions on the right of establishment cannot be used to regulate anything else. On the other hand, the scope of these legal bases is wider than one would expect, because everything related to the subject can be regulated on these bases. The extensive network of rules implementing the free movement of workers can serve as an example.

The third kind of legal bases, those tied to the internal market and the objectives of the Treaty, also have a scope which was widened unexpectedly. The legal bases empowering the Community to issue legislation to establish the internal market and to achieve the objectives of the Treaty are laid down in articles 100 and 100A and 235 of the Treaty.

Article 100 provides for the power to issue directives for the approximation of the national legal or administrative provisions which directly influence the establishment and the functioning of the common market. Inserted by the European Single Act, article 100A provides for the power to adopt measures for the approximation of the provisions laid down by law, regulation or administrative action of the member states and which have as their object the establishment and functioning of the internal market.[14] The differences between the articles are threefold. First, article 100 prescribes the use of the device of the directive, while article 100A allows the use of all kinds of devices. Second, article 100A refers to the common market in general, while article 100A is restricted to the implementation of the internal market as defined in article 7A.[15] Whether this difference is of great importance has to be doubted. More important are the subjects specifically excluded in article 100A, such as the rights and interests of workers. If harmonization legislation concerning these subjects is promulgated, the legal basis of article 100 must be used. Third, decisions taken on the basis of article 100 should be made unanimously, while article 100A provides for decision making by qualified majority. The procedure laid down in article 100A is more democratic; since the adoption of the Treaty of Maastricht the European Parliament can cast the deciding vote if it comes to the rejection of proposals. Article 100 only provides for an advisory role of the Parliament.

Originally article 100A was inserted in the Treaty to implement a catalogue of measures designed to complete the internal market, the so-called White Paper.[16] The importance of article 100A was therefore thought to be temporary. The article would no longer be used frequently after the internal market was completed. Whether this expectation will prove to be justified depends on the view the Community and the member states take on the concept of completion.

So the limits of the legislative powers distributed by articles 100 and

100A are to be found only in the concepts of the common market and the internal market (from now on both will be referred to as 'internal market'), which are rather vague.[17]

The internal market comprises the free movement of goods, persons (workers and the right of establishment), services and capital.[18] These 'four freedoms' are of enormous importance in Community law. Although these freedoms originally had an economic objective, the judgments of the Court of Justice increased their importance to the extent that they can be compared with fundamental human rights.

According to the case-law of the Court of Justice, the Treaty provisions concerning the four freedoms are applicable if a case concerning trade, workers, establishment of enterprises, the providing of services or the free movement of capital contains a transborder element. This doctrine applies to the directly applicable Treaty prohibitions of hindering and discrimination as well as to the harmonization provisions. This means that if the Treaty provisions on transborder trade (articles 30, 59 of the Treaty) or transborder movement of persons (articles 48, 52) are applicable to an activity of an individual, then the national legal provisions affecting the activity concerned are eligible to be harmonized if and when harmonization may further the establishment, functioning, or completion of the internal market as defined in the article. Eventually this will mean that the Community has the power to harmonize every national measure potentially hindering trade and the right of establishment, and every national measure either directly or indirectly discriminating against non-national workers or facilitating transborder trade or transborder movement of persons.

The Court adopted the doctrine of the application of the provisions concerning the internal market in cases in which a transborder element[19] is involved a long time ago, and has gone quite far in its position.[20] Especially where the application of the free movement of services is concerned, this doctrine has had some striking results. For example, since the Court has held that the free movement of services is at stake not only when the provider of the service moves to another member state but also when the recipient of the service does so,[21] it *de facto* brought intra-European tourism under the scope of the Treaty.[22] Thus, as far as the protection of the free movement of services is concerned, intra-European tourism is eligible for harmonization on the basis of article 100 or 100A. This means that the power of the member states to regulate tourism is reduced considerably, even though no one ever thought tourism as such would be covered by the Treaty.

The other legal basis related to the internal market provides for the adoption of secondary legislation with a more distant relationship to the

Treaty. Article 235 provides for the power to adopt measures which are necessary to attain, in the course of the operation of the common market, one of the objectives of the Treaty listed in article 2. The article is intended to be used if the Treaty does not provide the Community with any specific power to legislate. Thus, article 235 fills the *lacunae* in the powers of the Community. Since it is tied to the objectives of the Treaty, listed in article 2, it does not fill any gaps in the objectives of the Community.

From the power attributed in article 235 it follows that, if the subject of a desired measure falls within the scope of the objectives of article 2 the Community is empowered to adopt the measure. This is extremely important because the objectives are defined in rather vague and broad terms. Though the Council originally made only a limited use of article 235,[23] this approach has changed over the years. Since the seventies the article has been used to develop a range of policies for which the Treaty itself does not provide.[24] For example: the adoption of a directive for the conservation of wild birds[25] was justified by the objective of raising the standard of living! This reasoning led to an extension of the jurisdiction of the Community through the use of the power granted in article 235 which may be regarded as questionable indeed.[26] Until recently, however, member states and Community did not seem to care very much whether the Community was entitled to use article 235 or not, as long as they all agreed Community legislation was desirable.

And as if all these attempts to extend the regulatory powers of the Community are not enough, even more roads to extension emerged over the years, derived from the Treaty-articles containing a legal basis to issue secondary legislation. If secondary legislation is issued, it brings the matters regulated within the powers of the Community. The extent of the powers transferred to the Community in this way depends on the substance and the wording of the regulating measure.

The interpretation of the concept of the internal market as defined in articles 100 and 100A and the vague objectives of article 2 of the Treaty, in combination with secondary legislation based on those articles, has led to an extension of the powers of the Community which is commonly called the 'spin-off effect'.

Over the years, this spin-off effect has resulted in a veritable flood of Community legislation on subjects way beyond the expected powers of the Community. For example, case-law concerning transborder services such as transmission of television signals has directly led to a Directive on transborder television broadcasting.[27] Another significant example is the case-law concerning discrimination with respect to university fees[28] and the right of students to enter universities and polytechnics[29] in other member states. These cases have eventually led to a Directive on the right of residence for students.[30]

The interfering nature of the jurisdiction of the European Community may be illustrated by the case-law on national social security. The Community as such has no power to establish social security systems or to abolish existing ones. Nevertheless, Community law does already affect national systems of social security. When the Dutch government tried to convert the Dutch system of health insurance into a public social security system executed by non-commercial parts of commercial insurance companies, it was unexpectedly confronted with restrictions following from Community law.[31] Because the establishment of a social security system means the withdrawal from the market of services originally provided on a commercial basis (in this case insurance services), the establishment of a national social security system does affect the internal market as a whole. This is not to say Community law prohibits the establishment of social security systems. It does not. But since legislation to establish such a system imposes on the insurance companies a wealth of obligations which may hinder the internal market, the government issuing the legislation has to be absolutely sure that the established system definitely is 'social security', and not an insurance system which is in fact commercial but only designed to close the national market for foreign insurance companies. So because of the requirements the internal market imposes on insurance systems in general, member states are no longer the ones defining what is or is not 'social security' anymore. Instead the Community is defining such notions in this way.[32]

Although thus far the definition of what constitutes a system of social security is only to be found in case-law, it is not entirely unthinkable that eventually Community legislation will replace the requirements laid down by the Court. This legislation could be based on article 100A or 235 because of the simple fact that social security systems can lead to distortions in competition between the member states, insofar as the definitions of what is 'social security' differ between the member states.

As a result of the judgments of the Court, the powers of the Community have extended to the point that virtually every area of national law can be affected by Community law. Even non-related matters such as medical-ethical issues,[33] family law, and even the national concept of marriage do not remain untouched. The adoption of legislation on a registered partnership for homosexuals to achieve the same legal consequences as marriage in Denmark[34] and the drafting of such legislation in the Netherlands, are things which cannot be done without at least reviewing their consequences with regard to the internal market. Member states adopting such legislation, may be confronted with 'marriage' tourism by citizens of other member states with more restrictive legislation, which is not something the Dutch or Danish legislation intends to initiate or wishes to encourage. Though so far the Court has held that the concept of marriage depends on national law,[35] it is at least questionable whether a member state which does not allow 'marriage' between partners of the same sex in its own legislation is entirely free to deny the legal consequences of a legally concluded 'marriage' between homosexuals in another member state. This is even more so if those statutory 'marriage' registrations have consequences for financial matters and for the position of the partners in social security systems and pension schemes. After all, if a registration is valid in one member state, then the act of registration could be seen as a service within the scope of the Treaty. This depends on whether the registration may be seen at the same time as concluding a contract between individuals.[36] If so, member states denying the validity of such a registration might be held to hinder the free movement of services.[37]

Whether the Community will ever issue any legislation on matters such as family law and homosexual partnership is doubtful; the member states do not seem very keen on it. Nevertheless it must be noted that as far as harmonization legislation is concerned, the Community may be considered empowered to issue legislation, if the differences between the legislations of various member states prevent the internal market from attaining its full effect.

Another factor contributing to the extension of the powers of the Community is to be found in the case-law of the Court of Justice on the doctrine of the 'implied powers'. Implied powers are those powers without which the power granted originally would have no meaning or could not be reasonably and usefully applied.[38] To apply this doctrine a specific power has to exist. If the existing specific power does not explicitly cover the promulgation of all measures necessary to achieve its full effect, the power to take those necessary measures is implicitly assumed. The theory of 'implied powers' has been applied mainly in the field of the external relations of the Community.[39] According to the Court powers granted to the Community in the Treaty imply the power to negiotiate treaties with third countries covering the same subject as the original power.

Though the application of the doctrine of implied powers is logical and necessary to attain the full effect of powers granted, it can lead to an extension of the scope of the original power which was not anticipated. Following the doctrine, the Community may feel free to conclude a treaty with third countries regulating a policy area only partly regulated by a

Community measure, while the treaty to be adopted covers a somewhat wider area than the Community measure. The eventual effect is that the concluding of such a Treaty extends the scope of the internal power. This effect of the doctrine of implied powers will be illustrated by the implied power which will probably be used to conclude a Convention on transborder broadcasting within the framework of the Council of Europe.

After a series of judgments on televised advertising and cable television,[40] the Community in 1989 adopted a Directive on transborder television broadcasting.[41] Article 22 of this Directive prohibits broadcasting programmes which contain elements such as unnecessary violence and pornography, which may be considered harmful for children and adolescents. It also prohibits broadcasting programmes containing other elements considered harmful for children and adolescents at times when they may be expected to be watching.

The concepts of 'pornography', 'unnecessary violence' and 'harmful elements', however, are not defined in the directive. The member states must apply these concepts discretionarily, according to their cultural backgrounds. This discretionary freedom is not uncommon in Community law; the interpretation of concepts such as public order and public safety is also left primarily in the hands of the member states. The case-law of the Court on these last concepts indicates there is some latitude for the member states here, as long as they do not discriminate against foreign nationals or hinder the free movement unnecessarily.[42] The Court probably will grant the member states the same latitude if it rules on an interpretation of the concepts in the Directive on transborder broadcasting. In that case, more freedom to broadcast programmes (containing sex scenes for example) will exist in one member state than in another, because of differences between member states as to what is regarded as pornographic.[43]

At the same time the Directive was adopted, a Convention concerning transborder television was being negotiated within the framework of the Council of Europe.[44] This Convention contains provisions which considerably limit the interpretation of the described concepts.[45] The Netherlands regarded these provisions of the Convention as too interfering with the Dutch view and therefore decided not to ratify the Treaty.[46]

However, the Netherlands may find itself bound by the Convention eventually, because the doctrine of the implied powers enables the Community to adopt the Convention. The mere fact that the Directive leaves room for the member states to conduct their own policy on this subject matter does not affect the implied power directly derived from the existence of the Directive on this issue.[47] If the Community ratifies the Convention, it is arguable that the Court of Justice is obliged to interpret the above-described concepts of the Directive in compliance with the Convention. Thus the freedom of the Netherlands to interpret them according to its cultural background vanishes, even though it never intended to be bound that way and even consciously tried to avoid being bound to such resticting measures. This extension of the powers of the Community is solely due to the application of the doctrine of implied powers.

Finally, the Treaty of Maastricht contains a novelty which makes it possible to transfer powers from the member states to the Community which are not covered by the objectives of the Treaty, without revising the Treaty. While justice and home affairs in itself are issues completely under the jurisdiction of the member states and co-operation between the member states is regulated in the intergovernmental part of the Treaty of Maastricht, the Council may, under article K.9 of the Treaty of Maastricht, unanimously decide to apply article 100C of the Treaty to those issues listed in article K.1 as issues of common interest.

Article 100C provides for a procedure concerning the decision about which nationals of third countries should hold visas when crossing the external borders of the member states. In principle, decisions based on this article should be made unanimously. The list in article K.1 contains among others: asylum policy, immigration policy (including conditions of entry and movement), conditions of residents, family reunion and access to employment, combating drug addiction and fraud on an international scale, insofar as these issues are not covered by the other articles of the Treaty of Maastricht or by judicial co-operation in civil matters. These matters are not yet included in the jurisdiction of the Community. Although article K.9 refers explicitly to applying the procedure of article 100C and refers equally explicitly to the constitutional rules of the member states for adoption of the application, one should not underestimate the impact article K.9 may have on the limitation of the powers of the member states in this field. When applying the procedures of article 100C these issues become part of the jurisdiction of the Community, at least as far as the decision procedure is concerned. This means the Court of Justice is the Court which may decide whether the provision is correctly applied.

Secondly, decisions taken on the legal basis of article 100C are decisions taken under Community law by Community institutions. According to the other Treaty articles, the Court of Justice is the Court interpreting Community law. There is no apparent reason why decisions taken on the basis of article 100C applied according to article K.9 should form an exception on this rule. So the innocent phrasing of article K.9 may lead to a substantial addition to the powers of the Community and an equally substantial loss for the member states in areas the member states have always considered to belong exclusively to their jurisdiction.

So the Community has an excellent chance to gain more powers, due to the vague objectives of the Treaty, the widely interpreted concept of the internal market, the doctrine of implied powers and the *passerelle* provision of article K.9 of the Treaty of Maastricht.

The powers derived from the legal bases in relation to the substance of the Treaty have already led to some anxiety in the member states. The member states feel the Community may be entitled to harmonize virtually every aspect of national life. To prevent this, the Treaty of Maastricht incorporated the principle of subsidiarity, which is meant to put a stop to an overeagerly harmonizing Community. The principle of subsidiarity does not restrict the transfer of powers, however, but only limits the use of existing powers. Therefore, it will not be discussed in this chapter. Because of its probable future importance (also in the legal field) the next chapter is entirely devoted to this principle.

2.1 Limits on the powers of the Community

2.1.1 The limits of the Treaty. By now, the innocent reader may be convinced that the Community is empowered to do everything it deems appropriate, and may be inclined to dismiss the regulatory powers of the member states as a relic from a distant past. This impression is wrong. Though the powers the Community has accumulated are impressive in number and scope, and growing, the Community itself is still bound to certain restricting rules.

First, the regulatory power of the Community is confined to the Treaty. The first limits on the regulatory power of the Community are the objectives of the Community as laid down in the Treaty. If an action desired by the Community does not fall within the objectives provided for by the Treaty, and no specific legal basis exits, the power to act cannot be attained through the use of article 235. In such a case the Community simply is not allowed to take any regulatory action at all. The second limit can be found in the wording of the different Treaty articles providing the Community with regulating powers. The power to act is confined to the wording of these articles.

Though this sounds obvious, these limits must be recognized to be important. One should bear in mind that, unlike other federations or states, the Community itself is not competent to revise the Treaty so as to attain more power. Article 236 of the Treaty only provides for an advisory role for the Commision in the revising process. The ultimate power to alter the Treaty still lies with the member states, and with every single member state at that. So the limits laid down in the objectives of the Treaty must be regarded as definite.

To explore the above mentioned limits one has to look at the jurisdiction with which the Treaty provides the Community and at the regulatory powers as provided for in the various legal bases. In general, the legal bases themselves provide the Community with the boundaries of its regulatory power. For example the legal basis in article 128 (the paragraph on culture), inserted by the Treaty of Maastricht, provides for the power to adopt incentive measures, but it explicitly excludes the power to harmonize legislation in these fields. So only those incentive measures which do not harmonize the national laws can be taken. But this restriction is again restricted in itself. The Community only lacks the power to harmonize those cultural matters which fall within the scope of article 128. If the cultural matters concerned fall within the scope of another Treaty article, harmonization is still possible.

This example is not a purely theoretical one. In some respects, the field of culture must be regarded as a market like any other. So if harmonization is necessary to abolish differences between the legislations of the member states which distort the functioning of the internal market, harmonization measures may be taken. However, this is not because of the power granted in article 128, but because of the power embodied in the legal basis of article 100A.[48]

Thus, the first limit on the powers of the Community can be found in the scope of the legal bases and in the general rules those legal bases intend to put into effect. Legislation intending to put the general rules into effect cannot go any further than the rules themselves.[49] To illustrate the effects of this restriction, I will primarily describe the general rules concerning the internal market.

As has been said above, the scope of the legal basis itself may be important for the kind of action that can be taken. Applied to articles 100 and 100A, this limit at once leads to some confusion. Articles 100 and 100A both confine their application to the approximation of provisions laid down by law and regulation, in other words the harmonization of laws. There is, however, no clear definition of 'the harmonization of laws' itself and no specific doctrine on which legislative activities constitute harmonization. Does the harmonization of laws require explicit adaptation of national legal provisions? If so, one may argue that it is not possible to harmonize through the use of the regulation, because regulations should not be transformed in national law, so the adaptation of national law should not happen at all. But since article 100A explicitly provides for the possibility of the use of regulations, one has to assume harmonization through the use of regulations must be possible.

The second limit is to be found in the general rule of the Treaty that the legal basis is meant to put into effect. The legal basis of article 100A refers to the internal market as defined in article 7A. Article 7A defines the internal market as the free movement of goods, persons, services and capital, thereby referring back to the rules embodied in articles 12 and 30 (goods), 48 and 52 (persons), 59 (services) and 67 (capital). As has been said above, some of these articles supply a specific legal basis; in that case, article 100A cannot be used to issue legislation. If there is no specific legal basis, the general basis should be used, and all measures necessary to effectuate the general rule embodied in the Treaty can be taken.

Measures based on article 100A cannot exceed the rules laid down in the articles comprising the internal market. This means the limit for what can be harmonized on this legal basis is to be found in the scope of the application of the general rules. For example, since the Court ruled that article 30 does not apply to certain measures of national civil law, like a duty to inform customers, because of its indirect connection with free movement of goods, article 100A cannot be used to harmonize such a duty.[50] If the member states feel harmonization is nevertheless required, another legal basis in the Treaty must be found. In this case, it could be the new article 129a section 1 under b, inserted by the Treaty of Maastricht, which provides for a legal basis for specific action on consumer matters such as the distribution of adequate information.

The general rules comprising the internal market also differ in scope.[51] Article 48 on the free movement of workers explicitly confines itself to the abolition of discrimination of workers from the member states on the grounds of nationality. The power is granted to take harmonization measures abolishing discimination, but not to abolish other hindrances to the free movement of workers.[52]

The rules concerning the free movement of goods and services as well as the rules concerning the right of establishment all contain a prohibition to hinder free movement. In principle this means that member states are not allowed to take any measure which hinders nationals of other member states in doing their trade, unless it is justified by a compelling reason of general interest listed in the Treaty itself or acknowledged as such by the Court of Justice.[53]

Harmonization measures may be taken to abolish these differences, so as to effectuate the proper functioning of the internal market. In most cases, these measures will impose obligations on the governments to provide for the mininum requirements for products, the standards for providing services, or certain minimum requirements that enterprises have to fulfil in reporting to the government. If goods, service providers, or enterprises fulfil the requirements of Community law, the member state is obliged to allow them on their territory.

Many Community measures do not prevent the member states from maintaining higher standards for producers of goods, service providers or enterprises on their own territory.[54] This is because the jurisdiction of the Community regarding the internal market is inherently confined to transborder trade.[55] Community measures do not in themselves affect the domestic situation in the member states.[56]

This restriction on Community law may lead to resentment on the part of nationals who have to comply with stricter requirements than foreign producers of goods, foreign service providers, or foreign enterprises acting in the same market. In a case concerning requirements for the size of health warnings on cigarette packets, a British company, who, according to British legislation, had to put warnings of a bigger size on packets sold on the domestic market than in the rest of Europe, protested that the British legislation put it in a disadvantageous position on the market compared to other European companies. Since the Directive concerned did not prevent Great Britain from taking such measures, the Court of Justice ruled it was not a case of discrimination under Community law.[57]

But, though it is inherent to the internal market to restrict the regulatory powers of the Community to transborder trade and transborder movement of persons, this is not the case for the legal bases providing for the power to regulate a certain policy area, such as the health and safety of workers or public health. The limits of these legal bases depend on the power provided for in the legal basis itself and the general rule they intend to put into effect.

Nevertheless, a more serious limit is to be found within the Treaty. The Treaty only covers the member states and their nationals.[58] Though under many rules non-Community nationals, residing in a member state, can rely on national provisions which were only incorporated in national law because Community law required their incorporation, their ability to rely on those rules does not follow from Community law but from the national law concerned. For example, the right of a Moroccan or American woman working in the Netherlands to claim equal remuneration, derives from the Dutch law implementing article 119 of the Treaty and the Equal Remuneration Directive 75/117 and not from Community law itself. Though a case involving a Moroccan or American plaintiff may even reach the Court of Justice (in case the national court feels the Dutch law needs interpretation under Community law), the rights of the plaintiff are not derived from article 119 of the Treaty or the Directive but depend exclusively on the Dutch constitution and statutory law. This limitation of the Treaty may lead to the discrimination of non-Community nationals in cases where this is unnecessary and unjustified. I will illustrate this with the system of the mutual recognition of diplomas in the Community.

Since the seventies the lack of mutual recognition of diplomas was felt to be a serious problem for the proper functioning of the common labour market (workers and free establishment) especially in the medical field. Since then, five Directives for the recognition of different medical diplomas were adopted. These were accompanied by Directives on minimum requirements for the vocational training of these professionals, so that a certain equivalence of diplomas would be achieved. The diplomas mentioned in the Directives must be accepted automatically in all member states and someone in possession of such a diploma is authorized to work in all member states.

Because of the partial harmonization of vocational training, one may argue that everyone possessing a diploma mentioned in the Directive should be eligible for automatic acceptance, regardless of his nationality. Whether he would be allowed to work and to establish himself in another member state, should only depend on other factors such as the question whether he would be eligible to obtain a residence permit. However, this is not the case. In Dutch law for example, automatic recognition of the diplomas is reserved for Community nationals. Nationals of third countries, in possession of Community diplomas, still need to apply individually for recognition and in this procedure the equivalence of their diploma is examined individually.

In other areas too, the limits of Community jurisdiction sometimes lead to bizarre results. Article 48 on the free movement of workers has been backed up by a Regulation,[59] containing a wealth of rights granted to Community nationals. One of its provisions contains, in short, the right for the worker to be reunited with his relatives. This provision embraces relatives with Community nationality as well as relatives with the nationality of a third country. It only may be relied upon, however, if the worker who invokes it has already made use of the rights granted by article 48. This means that if someone works in his own member state and never makes use of his rights under Community law, he has no right to be reunited with his relatives under the Regulation, while a colleague from another member state in the same situation does have that right.[60]

Though it is arguable that Community law is not meant to modify national law as far as the internal jurisdiction on these matters is concerned, it does not help the clarity and explainability[61] of the law. This is even more so since the Court has ruled that, if a person possesses the nationality of a member state, as well as the nationality of a third country, he should be treated as a Community national in every member state. Community nationality prevails even though the person concerned has always lived in the third country, has no ties to 'his' member state and has never even been there.[62]

Another consequence of the distribution of powers in the Treaty is that the Community in general lacks the power to impose sanctions on infringements of secondary law by individuals. The Treaty only contains authorization to enforce Community law in the case of violations by member states; since the Treaty of Maastricht was adopted the Court of Justice may even impose a fine on member states because of repeated violations. Violation of the Treaty or secondary law by the subjects of the member states is, however, a matter belonging to the jurisdiction of the member states. According to the Court of Justice, the Community is only empowered to impose administrative sanctions within the framework of the common agricultural policy.[63] The Court derives this power from the wording of article 40 of the Treaty which obliges the Community to adopt all measures necessary to achieve the objectives of article 39 of the Treaty. Apparently the Court regards administrative sanctions as a necessary measure. On the whole, whether in civil or in criminal law, however, the power to impose sanctions belongs to the exclusive jurisdiction of the member states.

This lack of powers of the Community leads to different sanctions in the various member states[64] which, it is argued, may eventually jeopardize the effectiveness of Community law. However, until now no attempt has been made to include the power to impose sanctions in the Treaty; also, no suggestion has been forwarded that the doctrine of the implied powers would cover an implied power to impose sanctions. One may even argue that the inclusion of the provisions concerning co-operation on criminal law between the member states in one of the intergovernmental pillars of the Treaty of Maastricht stops the Community from extending its powers to this area of the law.

Despite this lack of power the Court of Justice has ruled in various judgments that sanctions, though being a national matter per se, have to meet certain requirements so as to ensure the full effect of Community law.

In Von Colson and Kamann vs Land Nordrhein-Westfalen[65] and Harz vs Deutsche Tradax[66] the Court of Justice held that since national courts are obliged to interpret their national law in the light of the spirit and the wording of Community law, the statutory sanction which was too light, should not be applied. It ruled that '(...) it (was) impossible to establish real equality of opportunity without an appropriate system of sanctions'. Recently the Court of Justice ruled that member states may be under the obligation to pay damages to individuals, if the violation of Community law causes these damages and the provision contested provides those individuals with rights they should be able to rely on before the courts.[67] Because these last judgments are of particular importance in the relationship between the Community and the member states in those cases where the Community regulates by means of directive, this topic will be discussed extensively in Chapter IV.

2.1.2 Limits derived from general principles of law and human rights. While the limits of the Treaty itself are designed to protect the member states from Community interference which was never intended, there are also limits protecting individuals against the Community exercising its powers. These limits, which are specifically designed to protect the individual, are to be found in the general principles of law. Fundamental human rights probably are the most important of these principles.

Fundamental human rights as limits on the powers of the Community were first recognized in the Stauder judgment[68] at the end of the sixties. Before this judgment the Court had always reasoned that it was '(...) only required to ensure that in the interpretation and application of the Treaty, and of the rules laid down in implementation thereof, the law is observed'.[69] In Stauder the Court acknowledged that human rights must be considered '(...) enshrined in the general principles of Community law (...)'. In later judgments the human rights protected by the Court were defined as those rights which are recognized and protected by the Constitutions of the member states. Also, international treaties protecting fundamental rights, on which the member states have collaborated or of which they are signatories can supply guidelines which should be followed within the framework of Community law.[70] This reference to other treaties clearly meant to include the European Convention of Human Rights (ECHR), though not all the member states had acceded to that Convention at the time.[71] By now the Court of Justice has virtually accepted the rights laid down in the ECHR as rights to be upheld in Community law, while applying the limits to those rights provided for in the ECHR in the same way.[72]

The incorporation of human rights in Community law does not mean that every single human right protected in the Constitution of a member state is able to set aside Community legislation which may infringe it. This may be illustrated by the Hoechst case.[73] The German Constitutional provision concerning inviolability of domicile extends to business premises as well as private homes. While carrying out a verification based on article 14 of Reg. 17/62, the dispute arose whether this constitutional protection would apply under Community law. The Court of

Justice interpreted the principle of inviolability of domicile as only protecting private homes, because this is the protection most widely accepted in the member states. With respect to the protection of business premises there are, however, major differences between the national legal systems. Thus German enterprises were offered less protection against Community interventions than against similar acts of their own national administration. The judgment therefore was much criticized.[74]

The fact that the inviolability of domicile is also protected under the ECHR would have made no difference, even though the European Court of Human Rights has ruled business premises are included in the protection offered by article 8 ECHR.[75] By only referring to the ECRH as a set of guidelines, the scope and contents of the rights as laid down in this Convention are interpreted by the Court of Justice itself. The Court has no obligation to follow the interpretation laid down by European Court of Human Rights which interprets the ECHR.

Member states are bound by the fundamental rights recognized by the Community when they implement Community law, irrespective of the degree of discretion they have in designing their national measures. This follows from the obligation to comply with Community law in general. Since human rights form an integral part of Community law, member states are also obliged to adhere to fundamental rights while implementing Community law.

Also, when they take measures on behalf of the Community because they are authorized by the Community to do so, member states must respect the limits imposed by human rights.[76] Finally, they have to do so when they take measures in areas specifically regulated by Community law,[77] or affecting rights granted or protected by Community law.[78]

This last obligation means that any national measure which must be regarded as a permitted exception to the provisions governing the internal market may be examined by the Court with a view to their conformity with the human rights recognized by Community law. In a case like the Grogan case,[79] this could have led to an examination as to whether the Irish prohibition to provide women with information on the possibilities of abortion in Great Britain was an infringement of the right of freedom of expression as laid down in article 10 ECHR. Since the Court in this particular case did not consider the providing of information to fall within the scope of the Treaty,[80] this examination did not take place. Nevertheless, in his conclusion in the Grogan case, A-G Van Gerwen considered this question. He answered it in the negative, thereby concluding that the Irish prohibition of the information could be justified under articles 56 and 66 of the Treaty, which provide for exceptions on the grounds of public order, public safety and public health.[81] According to Van Gerwen, since these exceptions cover the justification of the prohibition, article 10 was not infringed. This is significant because the European Court of Human Rights later decided that the same prohibition should be considered an infringement of article 10 ECHR.[82] So if the Court of Justice had followed the conclusion, two (European) Courts would have interpreted the same fundamental right quite differently.

The position of the Court on the question of whether national measures should comply with Community fundamental rights, leads the present author to conclude that the Community as such should accede to the ECHR.[83] As we have seen in paragraph 2, because of the combined effects of articles 100, 100A, 235 and the resulting spin-off effect created by the case-law of the Court, many aspects of national law are by now affected by Community law. Thus, if every measure which may infringe the internal market can be examined on its compliance with fundamental rights, there are a wealth of national measures eligible for examination anyway. Since these national measures in themselves are also eligible for review by the European Court of Human Rights, it might be more economical to confine the ultimate interpretation of the same rights to one Court instead of two.

At this very moment we have the unpractical situation that two Courts, one based in Luxembourg and one in Strasbourg, may (and actually do) interpret the fundamental rights enshrined in the ECHR differently.[84] The result may be that the interpretations of human rights differ not only between the member states, but also between European organizations. That may jeopardize the idea that human rights are fundamental and universally applicable, which is a fiction Europe at least should try to adhere to.

If the Community accedes to the ECHR, the European Court of Human Rights might eventually become the sole Court to interpret the fundamental rights recognized in Community law. In that case, some unity on a European level would be achieved. When the disputed issue falls within the scope of Community law, the harmonization of the interpretation of human rights will also take place on the national level.

3 Distribution of regulatory power by delegation

If the Community has acquired a power it does not necessarily mean that all legislation on the issue concerned is promulgated according to those Treaty procedures involving both the Commission and the Council of Ministers. Like the member states, the Community legislator can delegate some of its regulatory power to the Commission or to the member states.

In this section the limits of the possibilities to delegate regulatory power in Community law are explored. First the author will focus on delegation to the Commission, thereafter delegation to the member states will be discussed.

Though it is arguable that the implementation of directives in national law can also be regarded as delegation, the present author does not hold this view. The power to implement directives follows directly from the Treaty. According to article 189 the Community is not allowed to choose form and method itself. In general, the directive as legal device for legislation is too unusual to fit within existing concepts like delegation. The directive as a legislative device will be discussed extensively in chapter IV.

3.1 Delegation of regulatory power to the Commission

Article 155 of the Treaty (and 124 Euratom) enables the Council to confer powers on the Commission by delegation. The powers are limited by the Treaty article itself: delegation is allowed only 'for the implementation of the rules laid down by the latter' (i.e. the Council). Implementation covers non-regulatory as well as regulatory powers, according to the Court.[85] Article 155 restricts itself to delegation to the Commission; in principle it does not allow the delegation to other administrative bodies of acts which may have the force of law.[86]

The limits of the regulatory powers which can be conferred on the Commission in this way are to be found in the word 'implementation'. According to the Court, the concept of implementation should be interpreted widely, because of the structure of the Treaty and for practical reasons.[87] The Court ruled that though the Council has to decide on the essential elements of the matter which has to be regulated, this does not exclude the conferring of discretionary powers on the Commission.[88] This means the Council may adopt framework legislation which can be regulated in detail by the Commission. Only delegation *'in toto'* is prohibited, because this would mean delegation of powers derived from the Treaty, not an implementation of the rules laid down by the Council.

If the Council exceeds this limitation on its power to delegate, member states may invoke the nullity of the provision concerned or of the entire regulation.

According to Kapteyn c.s.[89] there is no need to fear the Council's exceeding this limitation on its powers of delegation. They argue that rules laid down by the Council usually contain even more details than may be considered necessary. The Council explicitly desires to reserve certain powers to itself. When regulatory powers are conferred, the

Council often imposes obligations on the Commission to consult or even adhere to opinions expressed in the Management Committees or the Regulatory Committees in which the member states are represented. A Management Committee may even be established if the Commission exercises its power to implement the budget, if this implementation requires a substantive legal basis to take individual decisions. This in spite of the fact that the Commission is granted the exclusive power to implement the budget.[90] These restrictions of powers conferred through delegation point to a certain hesitancy on the side of the Council to delegate too much of its power to the Commission.[91]

Admittedly, very few cases concerning delegation have made it to the Court until now. A case which did make it to the Court concerned a Council regulation in which the power to prescribe specific sanctions within the framework of the agricultural policy of the Community was conferred on the Commission.[92] In this case the German government claimed that article 6(6) of Reg. 3007/84[93] and article 13(3) b and c of Reg. 3813/89[94] should be declared null and void, because these provisions contained a specific sanction against citizens.

The case was the following. In the framework of the agricultural policy the Community had established a scheme of subsidies for farmers producing mutton. To avoid fraud in this scheme, a farmer who committed irregularities in his request to receive the subsidy would be excluded from the scheme for the year following the fraudulent request. The member states implementing the scheme were obliged to impose this sanction.

The German government in general terms opposed the power of the Community to impose this kind of sanction, and more specifically challenged the delegation of the power to the Commission. Even if the Community has the power to impose these kinds of sanctions, the German government reasoned, it is a power to be exercised by the Council, not by the Commission. As far as the German government was concerned, sanctions should be regarded as essential elements of legislation which should be reserved for the legislator itself, because sanctions may interfere with the fundamental rights of individuals. The German government strengthened its claim by submitting that the principle of the constitutional state, in which a balance of power between the institutions must be regarded as fundamental, prohibits delegation of such essentialities to an implementing body.

As far as the power of the Community in general was concerned the Court ruled that article 40(3) and article 43(2) of the Treaty provide the Community with the power to impose all measures (including sanctions) necessary to implement its agricultural policy. Since the exclusion of subsidies may be regarded as an administrative sanction,[95] the Community was empowered to impose this specific sanction.

On the question whether the Commission could be empowered by delegation, the Court did not bother to explain its answer very thoroughly. It reminded the German government that the Council may only provide the framework of the policy; it is allowed to leave the details to the Commission. According to the Court, administrative sanctions are details.

The problem with this judgment is, of course, that the lack of democratic control over the regulations of the Commission is even greater than over those of the Council. From a democratic viewpoint, to include sanctions in such undemocratically adopted legislation is at least worrisome. The Court did not discuss this point, which was summarized in the German claim concerning the principle of the constitutional state. In the present author's opinion the reasoning of the Court to rule as it did must be regarded as rather thin.[96]

Another problem with the delegation of regulatory powers is whether the limits laid down by the Council in the delegating provision are correctly adhered to by the Commission. In certain cases the Commission itself tends to exceed the limits laid down in the provision in which the power is delegated. The following example may illustrate this.

Article 19bis of Directive 75/319 on pharmaceutical specialties[97] empowers the Commission to issue principles and detailed guidelines concerning the manufacturing of medicines. Based on article 19bis, Commission Directive 91/356 containing rules concerning good manufacturing practices for medicines,[98] however, does not only refer to the Guide on Good Manufacturing Practices as issued by the Commission itself, but also contains requirements for manufacturers. These requirements concern personnel, the manufacturing process, surveillance of the manufacturing process and even the requirement to introduce a system to handle complaints by customers and a system for the recall of products. In article 7(5), on personnel, the Commission requires the manufacturer to introduce programmes to monitor and ameliorate hygiene in the enterprise. These programmes should contain procedures concerning the health and the clothing of the personnel.

However desirable these requirements may be in themselves, one may wonder if all these requirements fall within the scope of the powers delegated. The scope of the Commission Directive is even more significant, because article 19bis only explicitly refers to the Commission with regard to the detailed guidelines. No other power has explicitly been delegated.

Nevertheless, no member state nor any Community institution has challenged the Directive because of its possibly exceeding the powers delegated. It might have been interesting to refer to the Court the question of whether the Commission could justifiably interpret article 19bis the way it did.

Delegation to the Commission still seems to be a precarious issue in the Community. The Council is not too happy to delegate regulatory power too easily and too freely. On the other hand, the judgment concerning sanctions points to a wide interpretation of the powers of the Commission once the Council decides to delegate. Since this case-law consists of only one judgment, it might, however, be too early to draw any conclusions.

3.2 Delegation of regulatory power to the member states

Delegation to the member states is not explicitly provided for in the Treaty, though probably it is the most common kind of delegation in Community law. Many Community acts provide for the adoption of implementing measures by the member states. In these situations the member states must be regarded as exercising delegated power. This is particularly the case in the regulation of the common agricultural policy, the collection of customs duties, and the Value Added Tax.[99]

In fact, when the Community issues regulations, delegation of powers to the member states is practically unavoidable. As has already been said, member states are not allowed to transform regulations into national law. Nevertheless, to ensure application in the member state, certain measures have to be adopted in order to implement the regulation. For example, in most cases the Community has no power whatsoever to ensure the observance of its regulations or to implement the regulation in general, so it has to delegate the power to the member states to do so. The same goes for rules regulating the apparatus implementing the regulation.

It follows from the nature of regulations that the discretionary power left to the member states by delegation is defined by the regulation. The member state is not allowed to exceed its power by adding to or minimizing provisions of the regulation. But even if the regulation does not define its limits specifically, the member states are obliged to ensure the implementation and the observance according to certain principles the Court of Justice has laid down in its case-law.[100] This means, for example, that the observance of the law should be ensured in the same way and with the same methods used to ensure the observance of national law. Also, the Court requires sanctions to be imposed according to certain requirements such as proportionality and effective deterrence.[101]

The effective implementation of a regulation in the member states also requires the use of administrative procedures, which are generally the ones already established in the member state. However, one must bear in mind that even if a regulation is implemented completely through the use of national administrative procedures, while executing the regulation the use of the national procedures is based on delegation to the member state. If the Community issues procedural rules in its regulation, these rules have to replace the national administrative rules, even if the Community rules are incompatible with national rules.[102] This may be the essential difference between regulations and directives; the latter ones should be implemented to form a part of national law while regulations providing for implementation only allow the use of national law as far as this is necessary for a proper implementation. This difference sometimes leads to differences between directives and regulations, which do not seem to make any sense at first sight, but are necessary nevertheless. The following example may illustrate this.

The prohibition to manufacture and market without a licence substances which are innocent in themselves, but may be used to produce illegal drugs, has been laid down in a regulation[103] and a directive.[104] The directive covers the internal market of the Community; the regulation covers the import from third countries. Both laws require implementation of the licencing procedures in national law. The general provisions of the regulation and the directive are basically the same. However, the regulation contains a provision allowing the member states to charge the applicants for a licence to cover the costs of the administrative procedure for providing them with the licence; the directive does not. On first sight it seems that the member states are not allowed to introduce charges while implementing the directive; only charges on applicants of third states appear to be allowed. This is, however, not the case.

The charge is supposed to form part of the form and method of implementing the directive, the choice of which is made by the member states. If the member state normally charges applicants for licences it can also charge the applicants applying for a licence as provided for in the directive, provided that the charge does not put a undue burden on the applicant which will hinder interstate trade. A licence charge within those limits is supposed to be part of the national administrative law and may therefore be applied. The directive does not need to contain a provision to enable member states to do so, the member states are free to do so according to their national law.

The use of national law while implementing the regulation follows, however, from delegation. The discretionary powers which the member states acquire derive from the power of the Community to regulate, not from national law. The Treaty does not leave any choice to the member states. Since a charge may hinder interstate trade and as such may lead to the regulation being applied differently in different member states, the regulation has to provide specifically for the power of the member states to impose a charge. If the regulation did not contain such a provision the member states would simply not be allowed to provide for a charge.

Thus, because the use of national law while implementing regulations derives from Community law, rather than national law, the Court of Justice is empowered to interpret the national law used to implement a regulation. One might argue that the Court rules according to the same doctrine when it comes to the implementation of directives. The Court of Justice requires the national judges to interpret their national law in compliance with directives when the implementation of directives is concerned.[105] The difference is, however, that the obligation imposed on national judges to interpret according to Community law follows from the Treaty and not from the directive concerned, while the jurisdiction of the Court to interpret the national law when the implementation of a regulation is concerned follows from the regulation. In other words, in the case of the implementation of a regulation, national law becomes part of the Community legislative act involved.

If the use of national law is a result of delegation, it follows that interpretation of this law when the implementation of a regulation is involved must be done according to Community law. This may result in differences in the interpretation of the national law between the Court of Justice and the national courts applying national law as such. These differences may affect the application of the national law directly, but they may also affect unwritten principles 'behind' the national law. Principles such as equity and good administrative practices may be applied differently or not at all by the Court, even though there is a tradition of applying them in national law.[106]

These differences in application of the national law have been an incentive to consider at the Community level the necessity of the harmonization of the application of the underlying legal principles of imposing sanctions in Community law.[107] A research project on comparative law in this area has already been launched. Whether this initiative will lead to harmonization of this subject matter, which is extremely delicate, remains to be seen.

4 Concluding remarks

Since the Community was established in the fifties, its powers have been unexpectedly extended. Areas which were never meant nor expected to be affected by Community law were deeply influenced by the effects of the internal market. The internal market and its spin-off did not confine themselves to economic subjects, but radiated out to policy areas which originally were not considered economic areas at all.

The extension of the powers of the Community as a result of this spin-off effect started to worry member states when Community measures seemed to be interfering with policy areas which are strongly rooted in the cultural background of several member states, such as some aspects of social policy,[108] culture, public health and education. Until the adoption of the Maastricht Treaty, these policy fields were generally thought to belong to the exclusive jurisdiction of the member states. Because of the impact of the internal market, member states feared that their specific policies in these fields could not be protected anymore without explicit limitations on the powers of the Community.

So when the Treaty of Maastricht was drafted some concepts were developed to prevent an all-too-easy transfer of powers to the Community. One of these measures was the incorporation into the Treaty of special paragraphs on these policy fields, in which the distribution of power was explicitly regulated; these paragraphs have already been discussed in chapter I. Another measure was the incorporation into the Treaty of the principle of subsidiarity.

Notes

1. Explicitly confirmed in case 26/62, Van Gend en Loos vs Nederlandse administratie der belastingen, [1963] ECR 1.
2. This was partly the cause of the American Civil War, see e.g. McPherson (1988), *Battle Cry of Freedom, The Civil War Era*, Oxford University Press, Oxford, 234-259.
3. For striking examples of this process in the United States of America see Tribe (1988), *American Constitutional Law*, Mineola, New York, 401-545.
4. Usher (1981), *European Community Law and National Law, The irreversible transfer*, Sweet and Maxwell, Londen.
5. Case 7/71, Commission vs France, [1971] ECR 1003 at 1018.
6. Case 7/71, *supra*; case 32/79, Commission vs United Kingdom, [1980] ECR 2403 at 2434.
7. Case 41/76, Donckerwolcke et al. vs Procureur de la Republique et al., [1976] ECR 1921; case 804/79, Commission vs United Kingdom, [1981] ECR 1045 at 1073 and cases 47 & 48/83, Pluimveeslachterij Midden Nederland BV et al., [1984] ECR 1721 at 1738.
8. Case 804/79, Commission vs United Kingdom, [1981] ECR 1045.
9. On this subject e.g. Krauser (1991), Das Prinzip begrenzter Ermächtigung in *Gemeinschaftsrecht als Strukturprinzip des EWG-vertrages*, Schriften

zum Europäischer Recht, Band II, Berlin.

10. On this subject e.g. Karpenstein (1988), Doppelte Rechtsgrundlagen im Gemeinschafstrecht, in Hess (ed.), *Rechtsprobleme der Rechtsangleichung*, Europa Institut der Universität des Saarlandes Vorträg, Saarbrücken, 55.
11. Case 45/86, Commission vs Council, [1987] ECR 1493; case 68/86, United Kingdom vs Council, [1988] ECR 855; case 131/86, United Kingdom vs Council, [1988] ECR 905; case 165/87, Commission vs Council, [1988] ECR 5545; case 275/87, Commission vs Council, [1989] ECR 259; case 242/87, Commission vs Council, [1989] ECR 1425; case 56/88, United Kingdom vs Council, [1989] ECR 1615; case C-131/87, Commission vs United Kingdom and Denmark, [1989] ECR 3743; case C-11/88, Commission vs Council, [1989] ECR 3799; case C-62/88, Greece vs Council, [1990] ECR 1527; case C-331/88, FEDESA, [1990] ECR 4023; case C-300/89, Commission vs Council, [1991] ECR I-2876; joined cases C-51/89, C-90/89 and C-94/89, United Kingdom vs Council, [1991] ECR I-2757; case C-359/92, Germany vs Council [1994] ECR nyr.
12. Barents (1993), Milieu en interne markt, *Sociaal Economische Wetgeving (SEW)*, 5-29.
13. The scope of the policy area may of course be questioned, e.g. case 131/86, United Kingdom vs Council, [1988] ECR 905.
14. The main differences between those articles are the kind of measures which may be taken and the decision-making procedure which in article 100A requires only a qualified majority. See Kapteyn, VerLoren van Themaat, Gormley (1989), *Introduction to the Law of the European Communities*, Kluwer, Deventer, 473-475.
15. The internal market is supposed to be more restricted than the common market. The common market encompasses the four freedoms (goods, persons, services and capital) and the common policies (agriculture, transport and trade) while the internal market only encompasses the four freedoms.
16. COM (85) 310 final.
17. For the differences between the articles see Kapteyn, VerLoren van Themaat, Gormley, *supra* at 467-477.
18. It is elaborated upon in the articles 30-36, 48-58, 59-66 and 67-73 of the Treaty and a lot of secondary legislation. See e.g. Burrows (1987), *Free Movement in European Community Law*, Clarendon Press, Oxford.
19. The transborder element is, however, absolutely necessary as the Court stressed in cases C-267/91 and 268/91, Keck and Mithouard, [1993] ECR nyr as confirmed in case C-292/92, Hünermund vs Landesapothekerkammer Baden Würtenberg, [1993] ECR nyr.
20. Case 186/87, Cowan, [1989] ECR 195; C-154/89, *supra*.
21. Cases 286/82 & 26/83, Luisi & Carbone vs Ministero del Tesoro, [1984] ECR 377.
22. E.g. case C-154/89, Commission vs France, [1990] ECR I-659.
23. Kapteyn, VerLoren van Themaat, Gormley, *supra* at 116.
24. For example a common regional and social policy, a common policy for

science and technology and common environmental and energy policies (see Bull. EC 10-1972, 14-20).

25. Dir. 79/409, OJ 1979 L 103.
26. Kapteyn, VerLoren van Themaat, Gormley, *supra* at 117.
27. Dir. 89/552 OJ 1989 L 298.
28. Case 293/83, Gravier vs City of Liège, [1985] ECR 593.
29. Case 24/86, Blaizot vs City of Liège et al., [1988] ECR 379.
30. Dir. 90/366 OJ 1990 L 180, declared null and void in judgment C-295/90 of July 7th 1992, [1992] ECR nyr; because of the wrong legal basis. The directive should have been based on article 7(2) of the Treaty instead of on article 235. The Court ruled that the legal consequences from the directive should be retained until a directive with the right legal basis is adopted.
31. Steyger (1994), Het Europese recht en nationale systemen van sociale zekerheid, *Sociaal Maandblad Arbeid*, Volume 49, 1 and 2, at 8-19.
32. Joined cases C-159/91 and C-160/91, Poucet vs AGF et Camulrac and Pistre vs Cancave, 17 February 1993, [1993] ECR nyr.
33. Case C-159/90, S.P.U.C. vs Grogan, [1991] ECR 4685.
34. Law no. 372, 7 June 1989, JLOV 1263.
35. Case 267/83, Diatta vs Land Berlin, [1985] ECR 567; case 59/85, The Netherlands vs Ann Florence Reed, [1986] ECR 1283.
36. Marriage in itself can be considered a contractual relationship, because of the mutual obligations established between individuals by concluding the marriage, even though the consequences are not negotiable but are laid down by law. If the legal consequences of the registered partnership are the same as those established by marriage, there would be no reason to deny its contractual status.
37. Jessurum d'Oliveira (1993), Lesbians and Gays and the Free Movement of Persons, in Waaldijk and Clapham (eds.), *Homosexuality, a European Community Issue*, Kluwer, Deventer, 307-316.
38. Case 8/55, Fédération Charbonnière de Belgique vs High Authority, [1954-1956] ECR 292 at 299.
39. Case 22/70, Commission vs Council, [1971] ECR 263 at 274-276 (also known as AETR).
40. Case 52/79, Debauve, [1980] ECR 833; case 62/79 SA Compagnie generale pour la Diffusion de la Télevision Coditel et al. vs SA Cine Vog Films et al., [1980] ECR 881; case 262/81, Coditel II, [1982] ECR 3381; case 352/85, Bond van Adverteerders, [1988] ECR 2085.
41. Dir. 89/552 OJ 1989 L 298.
42. See e.g. case 41/74, Yvonne van Duyn, [1974] ECR 1337; case 30/77, R. vs Bouchereau, [1977] ECR 1999; cases 115 and 116/81, Adoui and Cornuaille vs Belgium, [1982] ECR 1665.
43. See the written remarks made by the Dutch Government in case C-327/93, R. vs Secretary of State for National Heritage, *ex parte* Continental Television BVio et al., pending.
44. European Convention on Transfrontier Television, 5 May 1989, to be found in the Netherlands in Trb. 1989, 103.

45. Article 7 of the Convention prohibits 'indecent' programmes in a relation to pornography and 'undue prominence' of violence without referring to the probable harmfulness for children and adolescents at all.
46. Letter of the Dutch Minister of WVC (Social Services, Public Health and Cultural Affairs) to the Dutch Parliament (TK 1991/92, 22 300 XVI, 111).
47. See the Reasoned Opinion of the Court from 19 March 1993 on the implied power to conclude a Treaty within the framework of the ILO, OJ 1993, C109.
48. Case C-300/89, Commission supported by the European Parliament vs Council, [1991] ECR 2867.
49. See case 69/80, Worringham vs Lloyds Bank Ltd, [1981] ECR 767 in which the Court ruled that the Equal Remuneration Directive 75/117 did not exceed the limits of article 119. If it had, the Directive should have been based on article 235 instead of article 100. See also case C-93/92, CMC Motorradcenter GmbH vs Baskiciogullari, 13 October 1993, [1993] ECR nyr.
50. Case C-93/92, P. Baskiciogullari vs Motorradcenter, 13 October [1993] ECR nyr.
51. From here on, the free movement of capital will be left out of the discussion, because of its own specific nature.
52. The Court has already interpreted discrimination on nationality very broadly with regard to workers: see the already cited Diatta and Reed cases and case 16/78, Choquet, [1978] ECR 2293 in which the Court virtually conceded that hindrances were not allowed under article 48.
53. There is a wealth of case-law on this, on which I will not elaborate. For further reading: Burrows, *supra* (1987), Kapteyn, VerLoren van Themaat, Gormley, *supra*, at 387-392, 429-430, 443-452.
54. Only if the Community measure explicitly excludes higher national requirements is the member state not allowed to impose these. For example article 8(3) of Directive 73/239, OJ 1973 L 228, as modified by Dir. 92/49 , OJ 1992, L 228, on harmonization of insurances.
55. Timmermans (1980), Harmonisatie van wetgeving en Nederlands recht; beeld van bewogen beweging, *R.M. Themis*, 406-431 at 411.
56. Case 204/87, Bekaert, [1988] ECR 2029; case C-14/89, Nino et al., [1990] ECR 3537; case C-332/90, V. Steen vs Deutsche Bundespost of 28-1-1992, [1992] ECR nyr.
57. Case C-11/92, R. vs Secretary of State for Health, *ex parte* Gallagher, [1993] ECR nyr.
58. There is some dispute as to whether the power of the Community to conclude treaties with third countries on the basis of article 113 of the Treaty (common commercial policy) could affect the autonomy of the member states with regards to the rights and the position of nationals of third countries. See the Request by the Commission of the European Communities for an Opinion under article 228 of the Treaty concerning the WTO-agreements, which specifically adresses the question of whether the Commission is empowered to conclude the General Agreement on Trade in

Services, with the exclusion of the member states. Opinion 1/94, 15 November 1994, [1994] ECR nyr.

59. Reg. 1612/68, JO 1967 L 257 (also JO 1968 L 195).
60. Cases 35 and 36/82, Morson and Jhanjan, [1982] ECR 3723.
61. Though 'explainability' may not be a requirement for justice, it may be necessary to achieve acceptance of the law by the general population. In the Netherlands 'explainability' has been used as an argument for the drafting of legislation containing general rules on administrative law, see e.g. Verheij (1990), Naar een wetboek van bestuursrecht, in Verheij, Heringa (eds.), *Publiekrechtelijke bewegingen*, Kluwer, Deventer, 83.
62. Case C-369/90, Micheletti vs Delegación del Gobierno en Cantabria, of 7-7-1992, [1992] ECR nyr.
63. C-240/90, Germany vs Commission, 27-10-1992 [1992] ECR nyr.
64. Mortelmans (1993), De toepassing en handhaving van het gemeenschapsrecht door het nationaal bestuursrecht, in Vervaele (ed.), *Bestuursrechtelijke toepassing en handhaving van gemeenschapsrecht in Nederland*, Kluwer, Deventer, 13.
65. Case 14/83, [1984] ECR 1891.
66. Case 79/83, [1984] ECR 1921.
67. Cases C-6/90 and C-9/90, Andrea Francovich and Daniela Bonifaci vs Italian Republic, [1991] ECR I-5357. The extent of this judgment is not yet clear, see joined cases C-46/93 and C-48/93, Brasserie du pêcheur and Factortame III, pending.
68. Case 29/69, Erich Stauder vs Stadt Ulm Socialamt, [1969] ECR 419.
69. Case 1/58, Stork vs High Authority, [1959] ECR 17; see also joined cases 36-38 and 40/59, Ruhrkolengesellschaft, [1960] ECR 423 and on the EEC-Treaty case 40/64, Marcello Scarlate et al. vs Commission, [1965] ECR 215.
70. Case 4/73, Nold vs Commission, [1974] ECR 491; case 44/79, Hauer vs Rheinland-Pfalz, [1979] ECR 3727. See on this development in the case-law of the Court Betten (1985), *The Right to Strike in Community Law*, North Holland, The Hague, 27-45.
71. Pescatore (1968), Les droits de l'homme et l'integration européen, *Cahiers de droit européen*, 629-672.
72. Case 136/79, Panasonic, [1980] ECR 2033.
73. Joined cases 46/87 and 227/88, Hoechst, [1989] ECR 2959.
74. De Witte (1991), Community Law and National Constitutional Values, *Legal Issues of European Integration*, 1991/2, 11, claims the Court opts for protection at the lowest common denominator.
75. ECHR 30 March 1989, Chappell, Publ. ECHR Series A, Vol. 152; ECHR 16 December 1992, Steinmetz, Publ. ECHR Series A, Vol. 251-B. See also Cath (1991), Hebben ondernemingen recht op bescherming van de privésfeer? De zaken Hoechst en Chappell vergeleken, *NJCM-bulletin*, 28.
76. Temple Lang (1991), The sphere in which Member States are obliged to comply with the General Principles of Law and Community Fundamental Rights Principles, *Legal Issues of European Integration*, 1991/2, 23-25.

77. Case 222/84, Johnston vs RUC, [1986] ECR 1651; case 43/75, Defrenne vs Sabena, [1976] ECR 455.
78. Case 12/86, Demirel, [1987] ECR 3719; case C-260/89, ERT, [1991] ECR 2925.
79. Case C-159/90, S.P.U.C. vs Grogan, [1991] ECR 4685.
80. There was no need for the Court of Justice to go into this issue because the Court ruled that since the fact of the absence of a link between the information providers and the abortion clinics was established, there was no infringement of article 59 of the Treaty.
81. Conclusion of 11 June 1991 in case C-159/90, *supra*.
82. ECHR 29 October 1992, Publ. ECHR Series A, Vol. 246.
83. Sevinga (1991), EG, Grondrechten en grondwet, *Nederlands Juristenblad*, 1667.
84. See the joined cases 46/87 and 227/88, Hoechst, [1989] ECR 2959 and ECHR 30 March 1989, Chappel, Publ. ECHR Series A, Vol. 152.
85. Case 25/70, Einfuhr und Vorratstelle für Getreide und Futtermittel vs Köster, [1970] ECR 1161; see also Opinion 1/76, [1977] ECR 741.
86. Case 98/80, Romano vs Institut National d'Assurance Maladie Invalidité, [1981] ECR 1241. On the delegation of regulatory powers to the European Monetary Co-operation Fund see Kapteyn, VerLoren van Themaat, Gormley, *supra* at 122.
87. On delegation under the ECSC-Treaty (which does not contain a provision concerning delegation) see case 9/56, Meroni vs High Authority, [1957 and 1958] ECR 133 and case 10/56, Meroni vs High Authority, [1957 and 1958] ECR 157.
88. Case 25/70 Köster, *supra*; case 23/75, Rey Soda, [1975] ECR 1279.
89. Kapteyn, VerLoren van Themaat, Gormley, *supra* at 119, 120.
90. Case 16/88, Commission vs Council, [1989] ECR 3457.
91. Kapteyn, VerLoren van Themaat, Gormley, *supra* at 180.
92. Case C-240/90, Germany vs Commission, [1992] ECR nyr, the judgment in the German language is to be found in RegelMaat 1993/1, 38.
93. OJ 1984, L 283.
94. OJ 1989, L 126.
95. There has been some discussion about the character of the sanction: whether it must be regarded as reparatory or punitive. On this: Vervaele (ed.) (1993), *Bestuursrechtelijke toepassing en handhaving van gemeenschapsrecht in Nederland*, Kluwer, Deventer; also Bleeker (1993), Verantwoorde communautaire sanctionering van het gemeenschapsrecht, *Nederlands Juristenblad*, 1009-1013.
96. See also Bracke in his note on this judgment, *RegelMaat* 1993/1, 46-47.
97. OJ 1975, L 147 altered by Council Directive 89/341, OJ 1989, L 142, the Directive which incorporated article 19bis.
98. OJ 1991, L 193.
99. Cases 213-215/81, Norddeutsches Vieh und Fleischkontor Herbert Will et al. vs Bundesanstalt für Landeswirtschaftliche Marktordnung, [1982] ECR 3583.

100. De Moor-van Vugt (1993), Hobbels bij de rechtshandhaving, in Vervaele (ed.) (1993), *Bestuursrechtelijke toepassing en handhaving van gemeenschapsrecht in Nederland*, Kluwer, Deventer, 83-105.
101. Case 50/76, Produktschap voor Siergewassen, [1977] ECR 137; case 68/88, Commission vs Greece, [1989] ECR 2965.
102. Of course without violation of the limits of the Community powers as described in section 2.1.
103. Reg. 3677/90, OJ 1990 L 357.
104. Directive 92/109, OJ 1992 L 370.
105. Case 51/76, VNO, [1977] ECR 113; case 38/77, ENKA, [1977] ECR 2203; case 80/86, Kolpinghuis, [1987] ECR 3969.
106. Case C-377/89, Cotter and McDermott, [1991] ECR I-1155; see also the difference between the application of the principle of trust in the administration in case 316/86, Jonas vs Krücken, [1988] ECR 2213 and in the Dutch CRvB 27 June 1990, AB 1991, 55; 14 November 1990, AB 1991, 75.
107. Vervaele, (1993) Administrative sanctiebevoegdheden van en in de Gemeenschap. Naar een systeem van administrative bestuurssancties?, in Vervaele (ed.) (1993), *Bestuursrechtelijke toepassing en handhaving van gemeenschapsrecht in Nederland*, Kluwer, Deventer, 202-211.
108. Especially the role of the trade unions in industrial relations and worker particpation in the enterprise, see e.g. Steyger (1990), *Medezeggenschap bij veiligheid en gezondheid: de Europese regelingen*, Kluwer, Deventer, Chapter II.

III Drawing the battle lines

Subsidiarity and the division of powers between the Community and the member states

1 Introduction

After the Treaty of Maastricht,[1] which was meant to be a great step forward in the process of European integration, was rejected by the Danes in a referendum of June 2, 1992, for a while the Community institutions and the member states appeared to be at a loss in which direction the Community should move. Since it was generally believed[2] that the Danes rejected the Treaty because they feared that the Community was becoming too powerful, the other member states immediately started to clamour for restrictions on the powers of the European Commission and the so-called Eurocracy.

In response, the Community institutions pointed toward the principle of subsidiarity, newly embedded in the Treaty of Maastricht. Subsidiarity should quell the fears for a Community which is Big-brothering too much.[3] The principle was intended as a criterion for dividing the use of powers between the European Community and the member states in areas in which they have concurrent jurisdiction. Document after document was produced by the institutions and member states, describing how the principle should be applied in the different policy areas in which the Community has jurisdiction.

The areas concerned are already plentiful and their number will increase now that the Maastricht Treaty has inserted paragraphs on, among other things, public health and cultural and education policy. The principle of subsidiarity should enable the Community and the member states to have an equal say in formulating a European policy on these matters. Within the limits of the Treaty, subsidiarity should determine whether, when, and to what extent the Community may act.

In this chapter the author intends to explore the principle of subsidiarity from a legal point of view. Though one might argue that subsidiarity is primarily a political principle[4], its incorporation into the Treaty elevates it to a legal principle, which will have its consequences within the legal order of the Community.

The incorporation of the principle in article 3B of the Treaty may raise questions concerning its applicability in the different policy fields and its relation to the system of limited legislative powers of the Community. Furthermore the relation between the specific legal bases of certain sectoral policies and article 3B, which governs all powers under the Maastricht Treaty, might lead to questions. The most important question is whether article 3B will ensure an effective division of powers within the Community without disrupting the process of integration.

When discussing these questions, one must realize that the panic-induced interpretation of the principle which results from the Danish rejection of 'Maastricht' is not the only interpretation possible. The principle of subsidiarity is not just a means to restrict the powers of the Community; it also explicitly allows the Community to use its powers when necessary.

The principle of subsidiarity should be seen as a strengthening of the federal character of the Treaty.[5] In this chapter, the author will first discuss its consequences with regard to the distribution of powers. Thereafter the possibilities for applying the principle within different policy fields will be considered. Finally, special attention will be paid to the newly incorporated policy fields and the role of article 235 in relation to the principle of subsidiarity.

2 The principle of subsidiarity as laid down in article 3B

The principle of subsidiarity is a concept which aims to distribute powers in such a way as to ensure that administration will be on the level which is nearest to the individual.[6] The concept was developed by Thomas Aquinas to define the relationship between Church and State,[7] and in the Roman Catholic Church references to the concept are to be found through the ages.[8] Within the Community, adoption of the principle of subsidiarity has been advocated since the early eighties;[9] it formed a part of the original draft of a Treaty for a European Union proposed by the European Parliament in 1984.[10] The Single European Act, which resulted from this draft, did not yet contain the principle for the Treaty as a whole, but introduced it for the environmental policy.[11] So the concept is quite old and various theories concerning it have been developed through the ages.[12] However, the author will not dwell on its history,[13] but focus on its inclusion in the Maastricht Treaty.[14]

Article 3B of the Maastricht Treaty, in which the principle is formulated, reads as follows:

> 'The Community shall act within the limits of the powers conferred upon it by this Treaty and of the objectives assigned to it therein.
>
> In areas which do not fall within its exclusive jurisdiction, the Community shall take action, in accordance with the principle of subsidiarity, only if and insofar as the objectives of the proposed action cannot be sufficiently achieved by the Member States and can therefore, by reason of the scale and effects of the proposed action, be better achieved by the Community.
>
> Any action by the Community shall not go beyond what is necessary to achieve the objectives of the Treaty.'

The first subsection of the article is stating the obvious. Though, as described in Chapter II, the objectives of the Treaty have been stretched remarkably in the past, neither the Community's institutions nor doctrine have defended the view that Community powers could move beyond the limits of the Treaty. To incorporate this subsection in the Treaty was entirely unnecessary.

Where the division of powers is concerned, the second subsection is the most important one. Its application is limited to those areas which do not belong to the exclusive jurisdiction of the Community. This limitation is logical. If an area does belong to the exclusive jurisdiction of the Community, the member states are not allowed to act at will anymore, so no question of division of power arises and the principle of subsidiarity cannot be applied.

This second subsection, however, makes it more important than before to determine which areas do belong to the exclusive jurisdiction of the Community. Because of the nature of the distribution of powers in the Community, this determination will take place within the structure of the limited powers explicitly provided for by the Treaty. The question of whether a power belongs to the exclusive jurisdiction of the Community depends on the legal basis on which it is based. Thus, the legal basis on which a secondary law is based will become even more important than it is now. Already, Community institutions and member states are preparing the battlegrounds with regards to the meaning of the term 'exclusive jurisdiction'. While preparing policy documents to influence the outcome of discussions on the possible meaning of this term, they try to ensure a favourable interpretation.[15] The meaning of the term 'exclusive jurisdiction' may be determined from the case-law of the Court of Justice as it stands at this moment; that definition will be discussed below.

Another question is whether the Community is obliged to act when it is determined that the objectives of an action can be better achieved by the Community.[16] It is arguable that this might be the case, if the application of article 3B results in a conclusion in favour of Community action. One might reason that this obligation to act follows from the precise moment when the question of applying article 3B arises.

This reasoning goes as follows. Discussion about the applicability of article 3B should arise only when it is agreed that an action, either on the national or the Community level, is required. This does not follow from article 3B itself, but from the restraint every legislating body should maintain. If the problem concerned is not important enough to regulate, if government law-making will not solve the problem, or if the problem can be solved without government interference, there should be no action at all. This means that some research has to be done about the extent and the nature of a problem and the necessity of government interference before any action is taken.

In case no government action is required, the question of the applicability of article 3B should not arise. On the other hand, when government action is necessary to solve the problem, and it is determined within the limits of article 3B that the Community could achieve the desired objective more effectively than the member states, one might reason that the Community is obliged to act.

The phrase 'the Community shall take action (...) only if (....)' in the second subsection seems to preclude this interpretation.[17] It indicates that article 3B recognizes a freedom to act, not an obligation.[18] In the present author's opinion, article 3B should be read as only containing a political and not a legal obligation on this point. Otherwise the inaction of the Community might be considered neglect under article 175.[19] It is highly doubtful whether this would be a desirable result.[20]

The third subsection aims to incorporate the principle of proportionality with regard to the nature and intensity of the Community action. This subsection applies whether or not the action is within the Community's exclusive juridiction. It could be used to restrain Community actions in two ways.

First, it gives a rule to determine which legal instrument should be used if a Treaty provision does not prescribe the use of a particular instrument. On the basis of this subsection, the Council maintains that the form of any Community action should be as light as possible.[21] The

Council feels that, whenever possible, non-binding actions are preferable over binding actions, and the use of directives is preferable over the use of regulations. The Council acknowledged, however, that general rules for the application of this subsection are hard to provide; in the Declaration of Edinburgh,[22] it stated that the choice of the kind of legal measure being used should be made on a case-by-case basis.

Second, one may use this subsection to achieve a form of deregulation. It is arguable that the third subsection may prevent the Community from taking detailed measures on subjects for which 'basic norms' (i.e. norms which state only the result) would suffice to achieve the desired result. Such a restraint in Community legislation may provide the member states with more freedom with regard to the method while transforming directives into national law and implementing them in their national legal order.[23]

The Commission will play a crucial role in the application of article 3B since it has the power of initiative. The Commission determines in the first instance whether an action is required, whether the Community is the authority which should act, and which form the action shall take.

In the end, however, it will be the Court of Justice that will interpret article 3B. Member states can ask the Court to examine regulations and directives and rule on their compliance with article 3B. The article itself is not expected to have direct effect,[24] in the sense that it renders contrary provisions inapplicable. However, in the present author's opinion individuals will nevertheless be able to rely on article 3B to question the legality of Community measures in the context of a preliminary procedure or in a procedure against Community institutions. If successful, such a challenge may render the Community liable to pay damages.

Under the second subsection, the Court will have to examine whether an action falls within the exclusive jurisdiction of the Community, and if not, whether the objectives of the action cannot be sufficiently achieved by the member states. This second test especially may not be an easy one, since the provision concerned gives only an abstract principle.[25] It is virtually impossible for the Court to review in substance whether the objectives of an action proposed or taken by the Community could be achieved better if and when the member states would regulate the subject matter themselves. Thus for judicial review the reasoning behind the action of the Community legislator might become very important.[26] If the necessity of an action on the Community level is not justified properly, the action might be considered *ultra vires* with regard to article 3B(2). However, it may be argued that a Community action does not lose its validity only because the Community legislator neglects to provide a proper justification. In that case the only position the Court can take is to review whether any reasonable thinking person would think the action concerned is regulated best at the Community level.

For the member states, article 3B(2) may prove to be a device with which they can challenge Community legislation on which they are outvoted. Presently their only option is to challenge the legal basis of the legislation in the Treaty. Since the Council has started to vote on the adoption of Community legislation by qualified majority, member states which were outvoted have already brought several cases to the Court of Justice on the grounds that those measures were based on the wrong legal bases.[27] Besides the question of the legal basis as such, member states may now challenge a measure on the question of whether the principle of subsidiarity was adhered to while taking the decision. A wealth of case-law on this may emerge in the future.

Though Community actions are also open for review by the Court under the third subsection, testing against this subsection might prove to be even more difficult. Kapteyn submits that this subsection should be read in relation to article 3(h) of the Treaty, which contains the requirement of the necessity for harmonization.[28] This relationship may prove important as far as the choice of the legal instrument is concerned. It is, however, doubtful whether this relationship may be as important for the question of the intensity of the Community action when the contents of the specific measure is concerned. The fact that harmonization is required does not say anything about how detailed the specific measure should be. If one accepts that article 3B(3) also covers the intensity of the action itself, this should require a test separate from that of the test related to article 3(h).

In the present author's opinion, it is nearly impossible to determine whether an action of the Community is going beyond what is necessary to achieve an objective of the Treaty. Such a determination requires not only legal insight into the Treaty itself, but also a knowledge of the effects of legislative instruments in general. These effects are important to determine whether a Community action is going beyond the requirements of the Treaty and the reasoning behind the measure. So if an action is to be reviewed with regard to the third subsection, the reasoning behind the choice of instrument will, in the present author's opinion, once again be highly important.

2.1 The exclusive jurisdiction of the Community

As mentioned above, with regard to the applicability of the second subsection of article 3B, the question of whether an area which requires action falls within the exclusive jurisdiction of the Community has become highly important. If an area falls within the exclusive jurisdiction of the Community, the question of whether the Community is allowed to act instead of the member states should not be posed.

The Commission claims that the common policies on agriculture, trade and transport, the competition policy, and the internal market in any case belong to the exclusive jurisdiction of the Community.[29] Furthermore, the Commission claims that if a power has been transferred to the Community through incorporation in the Treaty, this power is exclusive. This has been called the *'element fonctionnel'* of the principle of subsidiarity.

On the other hand, according to the Commission, there is also a substantive element (*'element matériel'*) which determines the extent of the exclusive jurisdiction. If the Community has developed a certain policy in a specific area through issuing binding measures which restrict or abolish the autonomous legislative power of the member states in that area, this policy area belongs to the exclusive jurisdiction of the Community. Thus, according to the Commission, the Community is not required to apply the second subsection of article 3B in any area on which it has issued legislation. This even applies to those areas which have been legislated upon as a result of the spin-off effect.[30]

This interpretation is not universally accepted. Not surprisingly, the Council favours a much more restricted interpretation of the term 'exclusive jurisdiction' in article 3B. Others even question the presumption that the internal market, as far as the free movement of goods is concerned, belongs to the exclusive jurisdiction of the Community.[31] To include the free movement of goods might lead to the inclusion of all sectoral policies which are related to the free movement of goods, such as environmental, social and fiscal policies.

To find out which areas do belong to the exclusive jurisdiction of the Community one should first examine the Treaty provisions. This examination should focus on two questions: which powers are conferred on the Community by the different provisions, and which kind of action has so far been taken under them? Then one should examine to what extent member states are still allowed to regulate after the adoption of Community legislation. From this examination criteria can be derived to determine whether and to what extent the Community has acquired exclusive jurisdiction. It would require too much space to examine all Treaty provisions *in extenso*, but the following criteria may be applicable.

If the Treaty provides the Community with powers to support co-operation between the member states, no exclusive jurisdiction of the Community can be assumed.[32] In this formula, the Community is only empowered to support what the member states are required to do. The same is true for those provisions authorizing the Community to take binding measures which the Community has not yet taken. A legal basis to take measures is, in itself, only an option to transfer powers. It limits the possibilities of the member states to take any actions contrary to Community interests, but in itself it does not provide the Community with exclusive jurisdiction. Only after binding measures have been taken does the policy area become part of the exclusive jurisdiction of the Community, and even then only insofar as the binding measure goes and is allowed to go by the Treaty.

For example, article 118A provides a legal basis to take measures on the health and safety of workers. The article in itself does not bring the issues of health and safety at the workplace within the jurisdiction of the Community. Until the legal basis is used to regulate in this area the member states are only obliged to honour article 5 of the Treaty, which means they are forbidden to take measures which could jeopardize the working of article 118A.[33] If any measures have been taken, however, the policy area regulated by these measures does belong to the exclusive jurisdiction of the Community within the boundaries of article 118A. Since article 118A only provides the Community with the power to issue minimum requirements, the member states retain the power to take measures going beyond the requirements of the Community.[34] So the power of the Community after regulating on the basis of article 118A is exclusive only as far minimum requirements are concerned.

This is different only when a Treaty provision empowers and obliges the Community to take all necessary measures to regulate a policy area. In that case one may assume that the area belongs to the Community's exclusive jurisdiction. The mere fact that the Community neglects to use its power has no effect on the transfer of the power as such. The case-law of the Court of Justice confirms this.[35]

When a Treaty provision contains a clear prescription, the policy area to which the prescription applies belongs to the exclusive jurisdiction of the Community insofar as the prescription goes. For example, article 119 prohibits discrimination between men and women in remuneration for labour. This prohibition brings the area of remuneration into the exclusive jurisdiction of the Community insofar as differences between men and women are concerned.[36] Even the Community legislator itself is not allowed to alter this.[37] Apart from the aspect of equal pay, the area of remuneration for labour itself remains, however, in the jurisdiction of the member states.

With these criteria in mind one can say that the internal market does indeed belong to the exclusive jurisdiction of the Community. Articles 12 and 30 on goods and article 48 on workers contain clear prohibitions, and though the language used in article 52 on the right of establishment, article 59 on services and article 67 on capital is a bit more ambiguous, the Court of Justice has interpreted these articles as guaranteeing free movement.[38]

Measures taken by the member states which affect the internal market are only allowed if the Treaty explicitly allows them or if the member state has a justifiable interest in taking that measure and that particular area has not yet been harmonized.[39] Furthermore, those measures can be scrutinized by the Commission and reviewed by the Court of Justice. Since the Treaty provisions concerned are directly applicable, these national measures can be declared inapplicable by the Court when violating the provisions concerning the internal market.[40]

It is a fact that the Court has left the member states slightly more room to justify hindering measures with regards to the right of establishment, the free movement of services and the free movement of capital than with regards to the free movement of goods. This difference does not result from an omission in the powers of the Community but from the more ambiguous language and the greater range of activities covered by the articles concerning the free movement of persons, services and capital and the freedom of establishment.

After harmonization, the only legislation which member states are empowered to take in the areas of the free movement of goods, persons, services and capital are measures which do not affect intra-Community trade at all.

The Community is empowered to harmonize national law in order to facilitate the establishment, functioning and completion of the internal market; the member states are not thus empowered. The fact that since 1987 the member states have had the option of excluding themselves from the effects of harmonization measures (article 100A(4)) does not affect the power to harmonize in itself. Article 100A(4) provides for a very limited ability to maintain national measures which offer more protection to the individual than the Community measure, even when the national measure affects the functioning of the internal market. Member states are, however, only allowed to do so in limited circumstances, and after the national measure is approved by the Commission.

In the present author's opinion, the Commission's claim that the internal market as a whole does belong to the exclusive jurisdiction of the Community and hence that subsection two of article 3B is not applicable, is well founded. Therefore, areas related to the internal market, which have been regulated because of the judgments of the Court of Justice (spin-off legislation), also belong to the exclusive jurisdiction of the Community, at least if these regulations are based on article 100A or any of the other internal market legal bases.

Now a lot of harmonization measures are adopted after judgments of the Court in which national protective measures are held to be in violation of the Treaty. In such cases member states often push for Community harmonization measures to retrieve some protection for the individual lost by the application of articles of the Treaty concerning the internal market. However, harmonization legislation resulting from a judgment of the Court tends to regulate more matters than the judgement itself requires. These matters will become part of the Community jurisdiction and can also be reviewed under Community law. So it has to be kept in mind that this spin-off legislation may have its own spin-off when cases about it are brought before the Court, adding more and more adjoining areas to Community jurisdiction. Member states therefore should ask themselves whether it is such a good idea to require harmonization after an unfavourable judgment has been issued. They might be better off when they just lick their wounds, correct the national law as far as necessary, and keep the area as a whole outside the Community sphere of influence.

'Spin-off measures' based on article 235 may pose a different problem, which may become acute if binding measures issued by the Community based on this article are going to be repealed, for example because of the deregulation requirement of article 3B, subsection 3. If a binding measure is adopted on the basis of article 235, it brings the regulated matter within the jurisdiction of the Community. The area as a whole remains, however, within the national jurisdiction. This follows from the nature of article 235, which can be used only if there is no specific power for the Community on the subject concerned. The difference between that case and a regulated matter considered within the boundaries of the internal market is, that if a measure based on article 100A is repealed, the internal market aspects of the regulated issue remain within the jurisdiction of the Community. Only the spin-off returns to the jurisdiction of the member states. If the Community decides to repeal a measure based on article 235, however, in most cases no part of the matter remains within the jurisdiction of the Community. The measure concerned had to be based on article 235, simply because no specific power to regulate on the subject matter existed. Thus, the area as a whole returns to the jurisdiction of the member states. So it might prove to be possible to curtail the field of Community jurisdiction through an act of the Community without changing the Treaty.[41]

3 The application of the principle in fields which do not belong to the exclusive jurisdiction of the Community

Without having any case-law to rely on, it is nearly impossible to predict how the principle of subsidiarity will be applied in practice. Policy fields on which the Community has a power to regulate but which definitely do not belong to the exclusive jurisdiction of the Community are scarce. The most clear examples are the social policy area and the environmental area. There has been some theorizing about the application of the principle in these policy areas.[42] These theories on this application might influence subsidiarity in the policy areas added by the Maastricht Treaty. Therefore it is important to examine these theories.

While examining these theories, however, one has to bear in mind that no case-law on the principle exists in the area of environmental policy and, worse yet, no obligation to apply the principle exists in the area of social policy. So if there is any conclusion to be drawn, it can only be provisional.

3.1 The examples: the social policy and the environmental policy

According to the criteria mentioned in section 3.1, the principle of subsidiarity will definitely be applicable in the area of social policy after 'Maastricht' is adopted. Since the field of social policy has formed part of the Treaty since 1958, binding measures on social policy matters have already been taken.

Of those issues which have been regulated to facilitate the internal market, one might argue that the necessity of regulation is quite clear. Social policy measures like the Regulation on the co-ordination of social security schemes are necessary to facilitate the functioning of the free movement of workers.[43] So there is no question of whether the member states could regulate this matter themselves in preference to the Community.[44]

This is different for those issues which have been regulated in the field of labour. It is not very clear on what grounds the regulated issues have been chosen. The elaborate legislation on the equal treatment of men and women may be seen as a logical result of completing the equal remuneration provision in the Treaty. There was, however, no reason to assume that the Community could regulate equal treatment better than the member states; member states could have regulated this issue as adequately as the Community if they had wished to do so. It has to be feared that the member states only accepted the equal treatment directives of the seventies because they could not reject the Commission proposals without offending a large part of their population. The case-law over the years has shown, however, that the implementation of those directives has been neither very thorough nor very timely.[45]

The Community legislation on collective redundancies,[46] the protection of workers in the case of take-overs,[47] and the protection of workers in the case of the employer's insolvability[48] has no direct relationship with the internal market, since these directives also apply in entirely domestic situations. The binding element may be found in the wider objective of establishing a common labour market in which competition between member states can not be achieved through reducing the rights of employees.

If this is the source from which measures on labour issues originated, the conviction that the common labour market should be a fair one was, however, not very much internalized by the member states. The proposals on worker participation in enterprises and companies have all been aborted until recently, regardless of whether they concerned the national or the international level.

On the other hand, a veritable flood of directives on the health and safety of workers has been adopted and proposed[49] over the last decade. If one compares the attitude to health and safety legislation with the attitude of the member states toward other measures on labour law, one might suspect that the willingness to transfer powers in the field of labour has more to do with the political acceptability of the measures concerned than with the question at which level regulation will be more effective.[50] The enthusiasm of the member states even went so far that they added a legal basis to the Treaty, which provided for decision making by a qualified majority in this policy area.

In the area of social policy, therefore, no concept of subsidiarity seems to have been systematically used to determine which issues could be regulated better at the Community level than at the national level.

It has been submitted that the principle of subsidiarity in social policy should be put into effect with the intention to achieve a balance between contractual and legislative matters.[51] The most important issue should not be the balance of power between Community and member states, but the question of what must be regulated by law and what can be accomplished through co-ordination by private and public actors or collective bargaining. Though the present author agrees with the suggestion that this choice between government legislation and voluntary regulation is an important matter within the social policy area,[52] it has to be submitted that article 3B does not regulate that choice. Article 3B has been written to achieve a balance of power between governments. If this balance is not in question, article 3B is not applicable. In such a case the question should be asked whether government legislation is desirable at all. If it is not, and the matters to be regulated are left to co-ordination by private and public actors or to the mechanisms of collective bargaining, there is little opportunity for the Community or the member states to influence whether those private and public actors, or the trade unions and the employer organizations, decide to regulate the matter on a national or a European level.

The environmental provisions inserted in the Treaty by the Single European Act already contain the principle of subsidiarity. Article 130R, subsection 4, says that the Community will take action relating to the environment in so far as those environmental objectives can be attained more successfully at the Community level than at the level of the member states. This phrasing seems to indicate that the power to regulate environmental issues belongs to the member states in the first place.

Opinions differ on the manner in which article 130R(4) should be applied. Brinkhorst argues that the principle must be seen as a guideline stating that action should be taken at the most suitable level, as long as it does not fix boundaries.[53] This point of view stresses the political nature of the principle of subsidiarity. Pappas maintains that the principle may be regarded as a legal principle. He feels we should trust the Court of Justice to deal with the political nature of subsidiarity.[54]

The discussion is blurred by the simultaneous discussion concerning the appropriate legal basis for environmental policy. Pappas derives his point of view from a case related to subsidiarity, but which is in fact concerned mainly with the legal basis of a disputed measure. The case (Commission vs Council), which will be discussed below, is therefore not decisive on the manner of application of the principle.[55] Nevertheless the judgment in this case is important because it seems to widen the scope of article 100A, and consequently to narrow the scope of the specific legal basis. The scope of article 100A will in the future determine the ability to apply article 3B(2).

The case concerned an application by the Commission, supported by the European Parliament, for a declaration of annulment of a directive on harmonization of the programmes for the reduction and eventual elimination of pollution caused by waste from the titanium dioxide industry.[56] The directive had been adopted unanimously by the Council, on the basis of article 130S, despite the fact that the Commission had based its proposal on article 100A. The Commission held that even though the directive would contribute to the protection of the environment, the principal objective of the directive was to improve the conditions of competition in the titanium dioxide industry. Consequently, it was a directive aimed at the establishment and functioning of the internal market. According to the Commission the directive had to be based on article 100A.

In its judgment the Court held that article 100A prevailed over article 130S if a substantive part of a directive deals with internal market issues, even if the aim of a directive was the protection of the environment. The use of a double legal basis was impossible according to the Court, since it would lead to a cumulation of legislative procedures.[57] The Court reasoned that the prevalence of article 100A was also necessary because of the more democratic nature of the legislative procedure prescribed by article 100A.[58]

Some authors characterize this as the most important element of the judgment and reason that if two legal bases apply, the one with the more democratic procedure prevails. Barents, however, considers that the democratic nature of the legislative procedure is less important. In his view, the democratic nature of the legal basis supports the outcome but does not make it inevitable.[59]

Barents inferred from the Titanium dioxide case that in this case the only reason for the prevalence of article 100A lies in the main determinants which form the basis of the judgment of the Court. These concern the internal market. In his opinion the main determinants for the legal basis are the considerations concerning the objective and contents of the directive.[60] These can be found in the preamble of the directive and are susceptible to judicial review. No other elements, for example the uncontrollable 'centre of gravity' of a measure, which cannot be found in the directive itself or the preamble accompanying it, should determine the legal basis. A later judgment of the Court on the legal basis of the residence directive seems to support this point of view.[61]

Since at the time of this judgment, the principle of subsidiarity was applicable only in the environmental field, the case has little relevance for the application of the principle in general. Nevertheless it may be seen as important with regard to the scope of the internal market. The scope of the internal market, and therefore of article 100A, automatically influences the scope of the other legal bases in the Treaty. An extension of the scope of 100A leads to an extension of the exclusive jurisdiction of the Community. Since article 3B(2) is not applicable when a matter belongs to the exclusive jurisdiction of the Community, the judgment might prove to be important for the applicability of this article after all.

3.2 *The principle of subsidiarity in the new policy fields*

The principle of subsidiarity is definitely applicable in the areas of educational policy, cultural policy and health policy. The legal consequences of these new policy areas are especially interesting, because the battles on the distribution of powers in these areas are about to begin.

Until now, regulatory measures in the educational field could only be taken on the basis of article 128 of the Treaty. Article 128 offers a limited power to regulate general principles for the application of a common policy with regard to vocational training. Though 'vocational training' was interpreted broadly by the Court of Justice,[62] the extent of the article was limited.

The ERASMUS and TEMPUS programmes for student exchange and the LINGUA-programme to stimulate language education in secondary schools, are partly based on this article. The limitations of the article became clear in a case before the Court concerning the necessity of using the additional legal base of article 235 for the ERASMUS programme. The Court ruled that the use of article 235 as a legal basis for this programme was indeed necessary to justify the exchange of researchers in addition to students within the programme.[63]

For the policy fields of health and culture, action could be taken only within the framework of the internal market on the basis of article 100A as well as on the basis of article 235. Within this framework an enormous amount of legislation was adopted in the field of health, especially on requirements concerning medicines, and the recognition of diplomas and vocational training for medical professions.

Though several cases on cultural policy went to the Court,[64] it never led to a flood of legislation comparable to that in the health area. The Community seemed to be hesitant to regulate the field of culture, even when it was possible within the framework of the internal market.[65]

As has been said above, the link these subjects had with the internal market worried the member states. They feared that the economic character of the internal market would endanger the national traditions which form part of the policy and the legislation on these subjects. However, to refrain from legislating on the Community level would have brought no solution. The Court of Justice increasingly ruled that the articles concerning the free movement of goods, persons and services were directly applicable in situations about which the member states had their national, cultural, and health policy hang-ups.[66]

The three articles on these policy fields inserted by the Maastricht Treaty provide for principles concerning the divisions of powers between the Community and the member states, thereby implicitly incorporating the principle of subsidiarity. Article 126, concerning education, divides the powers between the member states and the Community by transferring to the Community only the power to contribute to the quality of education by encouraging co-operation between member states and

> '...if necessary, by supporting and supplementing their action, while fully respecting the responsibility of the member states for the content of their teaching and the organization of education systems and their cultural and linguistic diversity'.

Article 127 on vocational training contains a similar phrase. In other words: no substantive powers in these areas have been transferred. Actions going beyond support and suppletion may be taken only on the intergovernmental level. How the scope of the articles 126 and 127 will be determined therefore depends on the interpretation of these terms.

In the articles concerning culture and public health the division of powers between the Community and member states is more diffuse. Article 128, the article concerning culture, has a dual nature. It prescribes that the Community shall contribute to the flowering of the cultures of the member states, while respecting their national and regional diversity and at the same time bringing the common cultural heritage to the fore.

The autonomous powers of the member states are not defined in this article; the expression 'while respecting their national and cultural diversity' is not aimed at a division of powers between the Community and the member states. It may only limit the extent of the powers of the Community itself[67] but does not provide for a clear criterion of limitation. Subsection two lists the subjects on which the Community gets powers to act. This list, which seems to be exhaustive, looks like a restraint on the powers of the Commission. However, if one considers the extent of the listed issues, it seems that nearly every aspect of cultural policy falls within the scope of the power of the Community.

Article 129, on health, speaks of Community contributions towards ensuring a high level of human health protection by encouraging co-operation between the member states. Apart from co-operation, this contribution has to be made through the lending of support to the member states if necessary. Again the autonomous powers of the member states with regard to these issues are not defined, though the subjects on which the Community acquires powers to act seem to be more restricted than in article 128. The powers transferred to the Community are directed at the encouragement of health information and education, and at the prevention of diseases, in particular the major health scourges, including drug dependence.

Though the prevention of diseases is a subject which can be interpreted extensively, this definition of the subject may prove to be important as a restriction. For example, Community attempts to interfere with the organization of health care cannot be honoured on the basis of this article because even with the broadest interpretation of article 129, the organization of health care cannot be regarded as prevention.

On the other hand, article 129 provides the Community with an incentive to take further reaching measures in the public health field. This stems from the obligation to co-ordinate health policy and the role of the Community therein.

All three of the new articles provide the Community with a legal basis to take incentive measures. This term is a new one, and it is not clear what it means. Nothing in the Treaty suggests that incentive measures cannot consist of legislation, whether through directive or regulation. With the principle of subsidiarity (article 3B (3)) in mind, it is arguable that 'incentive measures' are meant to be measures of a non-binding nature instead of legislation.

Subsection two of the health paragraph seems to preclude this conclusion. This subsection contains an instruction for the member states to co-ordinate their policies and programmes on health prevention. The Commission may, according to this subsection, take any useful initiative to promote such co-ordination.

The very words 'any useful initiative' in subsection two seem to fill in the vague concept of incentive measures mentioned in subsection four. Since subsection four provides the legal basis on which measures in the area of health can be taken, these 'useful initiatives' will be based on this subsection. However, nowhere it is said that these 'useful initiatives' cannot consist of proposals for binding measures which can be adopted by a qualified majority, according to the procedure of subsection 4. Actually, since these initiatives are meant to achieve the above-mentioned co-ordination, it will be very likely that these initiatives will have a binding nature. So by adopting subsection two in relation to subsection four, the member states accepted that in the health area at least some of the incentive measures may be directives or regulations.

These incentive measures are not allowed to result in the harmonization of laws or the regulations of the member states. This limitation is embedded in all the new articles. It was meant to restrain the Community from interfering too much in areas which are regarded as being mainly the responsibility of the member states. So only co-ordination should be possible. Nevertheless, the prohibition of harmonization creates its own problems with regard to articles 3B and 235 of the Treaty, which will be discussed below.

As far as the division of powers between the Community and the member states is concerned, the principle of subsidiarity seems to be embedded in the built-in restrictions on the legal bases of the new policy fields. The paragraphs clearly provide for a shared jurisdiction, which can be found in instructions for the Community such as 'encouraging co-operation between the member states and lending support if necessary'. This resembles the phrases in which article 118 of the Treaty (social policy) is formulated. On article 118, the Court of Justice has already ruled that since it instructs the Commission to co-operate with the member states, it does not affect the powers of the member states as such.[68] The difference between article 118 and the three new articles is, however, that these last three do contain a legal basis for Community action. Action in pursuit of the objectives of article 118 can only be taken on the basis of article 100 or, since 1987, on the basis of article 100A if the completion of the internal market so requires and if the action does not fall within the exception of article 100A(2).

This separate legal basis for these new policy areas is a notable difference with article 118, because Community action on the new policy fields can be taken without regard to the requirements of the internal market. This means that no transborder element is necessary as a requirement to act, not even an indirect one. The limits for Community action are embedded in the paragraphs itself and in article 3B in general.

Whether these limits will be an effective check on the increasing Community influence in these areas remains to be seen. It must be borne in mind that many of the items which, according to the new paragraphs, are excluded from harmonization do bear a relation to the internal market.[69] Prevention of diseases may easily lead to restrictions on the free movement of goods or persons.[70] By resolution, the Ministers of Public Health (meeting within the Council) have already stressed the relationship between communicable diseases and the development of the internal market.[71]

When the adoption of Community legislation on this subject is required, this acknowledged relationship might result in the obligation to base binding measures on the legal basis of article 100A and not on article 129. With the reasoning of the Court of Justice in the above-mentioned titanium dioxide case in mind, the choice of 100A as a legal basis for measures aimed at the prevention of communicable diseases can no longer be considered far-fetched. The new paragraphs differ slightly from the environmental paragraph because of their more democratic legislative procedures, but it is entirely possible that the titanium dioxide judgment might be applicable to measures concerning the prevention of communicable diseases.[72]

In that case, subsection 2 of article 3B and the restrictions of article 129 are not applicable to the measures adopted; the issue will fall completely within the jurisdiction of the Community. So to keep these kind of issues within their jurisdiction, the member states would be wise to avoid supporting these kind of resolutions.

3.3 The roles of articles 235 and 3B with regard to the new policy areas

A final question is whether articles 235 and 3B may prove to be important with regard to the policy areas of education, health, and culture. This question concerns the different functions those articles fullfil within the Treaty.

As has been said earlier, article 235 allows the Community to adopt those measures which are necessary to attain the objectives of the Community within the course of the operation of the common market. Article 235 can be applied only to regulate matters which belong to the objectives of the Community. These objectives are listed in article 2 of the Treaty.[73]

Since the new articles all aim to develop and protect certain areas, (education, culture or health), it has to be admitted that these areas do belong to the general objective of 'the raising of the standard and quality of living' as mentioned in article 2. If not, it would not be possible to insert these areas in the Treaty at all without adding them to the objectives of the Treaty. It would be arguable that article 235 would be applicable in these fields if the Treaty had lacked a proper legal basis, but now that the articles contain their own legal bases for specific measures, it must be held that article 235 is inapplicable.[74]

However, these legal bases provide the Community only with a limited power to take the necessary measures. In all three articles harmonization of the laws and regulations of the member states is excluded. Since the Community is not entitled to harmonize on the specific legal bases, the question arises as to whether article 235 could be used to take harmonization measures in these policy areas. The Legal Service of the Council has already answered this question in the negative.[75] It reasoned that article 235 can be applied only in cases where no powers to act were foreseen by the Treaty. In articles 126-129 a power to act for the Community is foreseen, but only the power to harmonize is expressly excluded.

The present author is inclined to agree with this point of view in general and feels that the use of article 235 for harmonization activities in these policy areas would be a circumvention of the expressly stated exclusion in the specific legal bases. However, this raises the question of whether this reasoning could be changed when the lack of power to harmonize is regarded in its relation to the principle of subsidiarity as embedded in article 3B and the principle of Community loyalty as embedded in article 5. As has already been said in the introduction of this Chapter, article 3B not only limits the use of powers by the Community but it also allows the Community to use its powers.

The relationship between these articles may become acute if a problem emerges which belongs to the scope of one of the three articles concerned while a harmonization of laws on the Community level is required to solve it. In such a case, according to the Treaty, the Community does not have the power to harmonize. On the other hand, article 3B provides the Community with the power to act if actions of the member states cannot sufficiently achieve the desired result. So the question is whether the basic principle which governs the Treaty as a whole prevails or the specific legal basis which limits the power of the Community.

Though one is inclined to accept that the principle *'lex specialis derogat legi generali'* also applies in Community law, a definite answer cannot be given. When one compares article 3B to other basic principles of Community law incorporated in the Treaty, like articles 5 and 7 of the Treaty, an affirmative as well as a negative answer is possible. Article 7 (the prohibition of discrimination on the grounds of nationality) has been held applicable only in cases in which specific provisions concerning free movement in the Community cannot be applied. This follows from the text of article 7, which expressly says that it does not prejudice the special provisions according to the doctrine of the *'lex specialis'*. Article 3B does not include such a formula, but one might say the *'lex specialis'* doctrine is nevertheless applicable here.

With regard to article 5, concerning Community loyalty, however, the Court has held more or less consistently that member states are not only allowed but in some cases are even obliged to act to attain the Community objectives.[76] So it seems that the principle of loyalty must be regarded as important enough to at least partly[77] overrule the division of power as laid down in the Treaty. However, this never went so far as to allow member states to violate a Treaty provision.

One might reason that in a case which requires harmonization to attain an objective provided for in a specific article, article 3B combined with article 5 could overrule the specific legal basis which exclude harmonization if failing to harmonize would jeopardize the attainment of the objectives of the Treaty. This reasoning could be supported by article F(3) of the Common Provisions of the Maastricht Treaty, which prescribes that the Union shall provide itself with the means necessary to attain its objectives.[78]

From that point of view, the exclusion of the specific legal basis would not be a prohibition, but a restriction which might be overruled if justified by necessity. Since article 235 already contains the criterion of necessity, the article might therefore provide an appropriate legal basis. In that case it would, to be sure, be imperative that the member states act unanimously on this.

If the exclusion of harmonization (as embedded in the new paragraphs on education, culture and public health) would be read as suggested above, this would not mean that the Community is provided with an unchecked freedom to harmonize. The harmonization measures taken and the reasons justifying it would be susceptible to judicial review. Community institutions, member states, and individually affected individuals could bring these measures before the Court through article 173 (application for annulment).

All this is, however, speculative. The answer will depend on how the Court will determine the extent of article 3B as a basic principle of Community law.

4 Concluding remarks

The principle of subsidiarity, as it is newly embedded in European Community law, may be regarded more as a political than as a legal principle. Nevertheless, it is expected to leave its mark on the case-law of the Court of Justice too. The legal impact of the principle of subsidiarity is related to the system of limited competences. The principle will most certainly induce the member states to pay increasing attention to the legal basis of certain measures.

Since the division of powers is regulated by this principle only in those situations in which the Community has no exclusive jurisdiction, it is relevant to determine the meaning of the words 'exclusive jurisdiction' and attach them to the appropriate legal basis. Consequently it will become very important to determine and define the exact aim of a legal measure in order to ensure it is based on the correct legal basis. The relation to the division of powers means, however, that the legal basis will more than ever become a political battleground.

To determine the correct legal basis for a measure is by no means easy. The member states and the Community will have to deal with the problem of the often unclear and ill-defined powers attributed by the Treaty. Whether a measure will be regarded as a complement of the internal market or an incentive in a specific policy field will depend mainly on the content of the measure and its objectives as stated in the preamble. The reasonings behind Community legislation may become increasingly important. This may be especially so in the new policy fields added by the Maastricht Treaty.

The member states may also find that it is not easy to implement the principle of subsidiarity in a legal system which has already existed for more than thirty years. In those years so much spin-off legislation has been adopted within the framework of the internal market, that to redefine the boundaries of the internal market may be very hard indeed.

To find criteria which will provide an adequate answer to the question at which level action should be taken may prove to be difficult. The existing policy areas do not provide any adequate guidelines: the haphazard way in which legislation was introduced in the area of social policy speaks for itself.

Subsidiarity may prove to be most effective in the newly incorporated policy fields. In regulating these policy fields, the principle can be applied to determine from the start at which level action should be taken. Even so, the member states should not forget that within these policy areas the Community is provided with new powers. The principle of subsidiarity may then become the last resort for the member states to keep within their power what they deem necessary.

In contrast to these rather negative conclusions, there is room for some optimism. Though the second subsection of article 3B may lead to wounding political battles, the third subsection might provide the band-aid. This subsection might lead to deregulation, thereby partly restoring to the member states what was taken from them through overly detailed Community legislation.

Notes

1. Treaty on a European Union of 7 February 1992, OJ 1992 C 191; entered into force 1 November 1993.
2. There is nothing to substantiate this belief; the Danish voters never justified their choice.
3. Not everone agrees that the incorporation of the principle was necessary to restrain Community powers, see e.g. Baehr, Van Hoof (1993), Burgerschap en mensenrechten in Hellingman (ed.), *Europa in de steigers: van Gemeenschap tot Unie,* Kluwer, Deventer, 58-59.
4. Barents (1993), Milieu en interne markt, *Sociaal Economische Wetgeving (SEW)*, 29.
5. Emiliou (1992), Subsidiarity : An effective barrier against the 'Enterprises

of Ambition', *European Law Review*, 383-407.

6. E.g. Brinkhorst (1992), *Subsidiariteit in het milieurecht*, Kluwer, Deventer.
7. Wolters (1992), Steen der wijzen ontbreekt bij subsidiariteitsbeginsel, *Official Journal of the Netherlands*, 222.
8. For example in the Papal Bull *Quadragesimo Anno* of 1931.
9. For an overview Wilke, Wallace (1990), *Subsidiarity: Approaches to Power-sharing in the European Community*, RIIA discussion papers no. 27, London.
10. See Steyger (1990), Vertrouwen is goed, controle is beter; bevoegdheidsoverdracht en democratische controle in pre-federaal Europa, in Heringa, Verheij (eds.), *Publiekrechtelijke bewegingen*, Kluwer, Deventer, 126.
11. See Brinkhorst (1992), *supra*.
12. On subsidiarity within its historical context: Emiliou (1992), *supra*, 383-407.
13. For a historical overview on the perceptions in the different member states, see F.I.D.E.-report (1994), *Le principe de subsidiarité*, Fédération International de droit Européen, Rome.
14. As for the political view on the principle in the Community see e.g. Delors (1991), The Principle of Subsidiarity: Contribution to the Debate, in *Subsidiarity, The Challenge of Change*, European Institute of Public Administration, Maastricht, 7-18.
15. Not only the member states are drawing the battle lines, the Community institutions are doing so as well, e.g. case C-70/88, European Parliament vs Council, [1991] ECR I-2041, on the question of whether a Regulation on radioactive contamination of food should be based on article 100A EEC or on article 31 Euratom.
16. Though he is not very explicit about it, Kapteyn seems to regard this as a viable option; Kapteyn (1993), De complexe rechtsorde van het Unieverdrag: subsidiariteitsbeginsel en nieuwe bevoegdheden in Hellingman (ed.), *Europa in de steigers: van Gemeenschap tot Unie*, Kluwer, Deventer, 48.
17. Maybe this is what Francois Lamoureux (Director of the Commission's legal service) meant when he said that '(...) this principle had more of a political nature than a legal one (...)' Agence Europe no. 5879 (new series) 14/15 December 1992, 6.
18. In the same way Kapteyn, VerLoren van Themaat, Gormley (1989), *Introduction to the Law of the European Communities*, Kluwer, Deventer, 115 on article 235.
19. Article 175 contains an action against failure to act where such a failure is contrary to Community law. This action is meant to induce action by the Institution that failed to act. It is only applicable when the Treaty obliges the Institution to act. See e.g. Kapteyn, VerLoren van Themaat, Gormley, *supra* at 289.
20. Until now the only judgment on an obligation to act has been in case 13/83, European Parliament vs Council, [1985] ECR 1513, when the Court ruled that the Council had to take the necessary measures in the field of common transport policy to comply with Treaty obligations.

21. Doc. EPU-417/92, see also Commission doc. SEC(92)1990 final.
22. Annex 1 to part A, Agence Europe 5878 (Sp.Ed.) 13 December 1992 and 58/8BIS (Sp. Ed.) 13/14 December 1992.
23. Steyger (1993), European Community Law and the self-regulatory Capacity of Society, *Journal of Common Market Studies*, Volume 31 no. 2, June.
24. Agence Europe, 58/8BIS (Sp.Ed.) 13/14 December 1992.
25. Kapteyn (1991), Community Law and the Principle of Subsidiarity, *Revue des Affaires europeénnes*, 35. More optimistic are Constantinesco (1991), La subsidiarité comme principe constitutionel de l'integration europeénne, *Aussenwirtschaft* 439, and Pappas (1991), The Legal Basis for Action to be Taken by the European Community in the Field of Environment, in *Subsidiarity: The Challenge of Change*, European Institute for Public Administration, Maastricht, 119-125.
26. Kapteyn (1993), *supra*.
27. Case 68/86, United Kingdom vs Council, [1988] ECR 855; case 131/86, United Kingdom vs Council, [1988] ECR 905; case 56/88, United Kingdom vs Council, [1989] ECR 1615; case C-62/88, Greece vs Council, [1990] ECR 1527.
28. Kapteyn (1993), *supra*.
29. Doc. SEC(92)1990 final, of 27 October 1993.
30. See section II.2.
31. Doc. brei 361/20044.
32. See e.g. the judgment in case 126/86, Giminez Zaera vs Instituto Nacional de la Seguridad Social and Tesoria General de la Seguridad Social, [1987] ECR 3697, in which the question of the division of powers was discussed extensively.
33. Opinion Court of Justice on ILO-treaty nr 170, 2/91 OJ 1993 C-109/1.
34. See Steyger (1991), Holt de interne markt de arbeidsmilieurichtlijnen uit, *Sociaal Economische Wetgeving (SEW)*, 616-620.
35. Case 7/71, Commission vs France, [1971] ECR 1003; case 32/79, Commission vs United Kingdom, [1980] ECR 2403; case 41/76, Donckerwolcke et al. vs Procureur de la Republique et al., [1976] ECR 1921; case 804/79, Commission vs United Kingdom, [1981] ECR 1045; cases 47 & 48/83, Pluimveeslachterij Midden Nederland BV et al., [1984] ECR 1721; case 325/85, Ireland vs Commission, [1987] ECR 5041.
36. See case 43/75, Defrenne vs Sabena II, [1976] ECR 455 on the applicability of article 119 and cases 80/70, Defrenne vs Sabena I, [1971] ECR 445, 69/80, Worringham and Humphreys vs Lloyds Bank, [1981] ECR 767 on the range of the concept of wage, and case 12/81, Garland vs British Rail, [1982] ECR 359.
37. Case C-262/88, Barber vs Guardian Royal Exchange Assurance Group, [1990] ECR 1889.
38. E.g. case 2/74, Reyners vs Belgium, [1974] ECR 631 (right of establishment); cases 110 and 111/78, Van Wesemael, [1979] ECR 35; case 279/80, Webb, [1981] ECR 3305; C-76/90, Säger vs Dennemeyer, [1990] ECR I-4221.

39. See e.g. case 8/74, Procureur du Roi vs Dassonville et al., [1974] ECR 837; case 35/76, Simmenthal, [1976] ECR 1871; case 120/78, Cassis de Dijon, [1979] ECR 649; case 174/82, Sandoz, [1983] ECR 2445.
40. See e.g. case 41/74, Van Duyn vs Home Office, [1974] ECR 1337.
41. As already cited in section II.2., in case 7/71, Commission vs France, [1971] ECR 1003, the Court ruled that powers transferred to the Community could only be restored to the member states by virtue of an express provision in the Treaty. This judgment does not cover the jurisdiction of the Community itself.
42. E.g. Brinkhorst (1992), *supra*; Pennings (1992), Is the Subsidiarity Principle Useful to Guide the European Integration Process, *Tilburg Foreign Law Review* 1992/93 Vol. II, Issue 2, 153-163.
43. Reg. 1401/78. OJ English Special Edition 1971 (II), 416.
44. Pennings (1992), *supra* at 161.
45. See e.g. Prechal, Burrows (1990), *Gender Discrimination Law of the European Community*, Dartmouth Publishing Company, Aldershot.
46. Dir. 75/175 O.J. 1975 L 48.
47. Dir. 77/187 OJ 1977 L 61 on safeguarding employees' rights in the event of transfers of undertakings, businesses or parts of businesses.
48. Dir. 80/987 OJ 1980 L 283.
49. Steyger (1990), *Medezeggenschap bij veiligheid en gezondheid: de Europese regelingen*, Kluwer, Deventer.
50. See Steyger (1990), *supra* at 27, 69-70, 276-278.
51. Degimbe (1991), The Social Dimension of the Internal Market and Subsidiarity, in *Subsidiarity: The Challenge of Change*, European Institute of Public Administration, Maastricht, 135.
52. Steyger (1993), JCMSt, *supra* at 172.
53. Brinkhorst (1991), *supra* at 91.
54. Pappas (1991), *supra* at 124.
55. Case C-300/89, Commission supported by the European Parliament vs Council, [1991] ECR 2867.
56. Dir. 89/428, OJ 1989 L 201.
57. Case C-300/89, *supra*, point 18.
58. Crosby (1991), The Single Market and the Rule of Law, *European Law Review*, 451; Sewandono, A. (1992), Beginsel van democratie versus milieu, *Nederlands Juristenblad*, 63; Schröer (1991), Mehr Demokratie statt umweltpolitischen Subsidiarität, *Europarecht*, 356.
59. Barents (1993), *supra* at 13.
60. See also the reasoning of the Court in case C-155/91, Commission supported by the European Parliament vs Council, 17 March 1993 [1993] ECR nyr.
61. Case C-295/90, 7-7-1992, Parliament vs Council, [1992] ECR nyr.
62. Case 293/83, Gravier, [1985] ECR 593; case 24/86, Blaizot vs University of Liège et al., [1988] ECR 379.
63. Case 242/87, Commission vs Council, [1989] ECR 1425.
64. Rigeaux (1992), *EEC-competence in the Cultural Field*, Kluwer, Deventer;

Loman, Mortelmans, Post, Watson (1992), *Culture and Community Law before and after Maastricht*, Kluwer, Deventer.

65. The major ones being Reg. 311/92 OJ 1993 L 395 on export of cultural goods and Dir. 93/7, OJ 1993 L 74/74 on returning cultural goods which were brought outside the territory of a member state in violation of the law.
66. Eg. Case 352/85, Bond van Adverteerders, [1988] ECR 2085 concerning public broadcasting and advertisement; case C-154/89, Commission vs France, [1991] ECR I-695 and case C-198/89, Commission vs Greece, [1991] ECR I-727 concerning professional tourist guides; cases 286/82 and 26/83, Luisi et Carbone, [1984] ECR 377 on medical services; case C-159/90, SPUC vs Grogan, [1991] ECR 4685 and the conclusion of A-G Van Gerven on abortion as a medical service.
67. See also the conclusion of A-G Van Gerven in case C-17/92, Federación de Distribuidores Cinematográficos (FEDECINE) vs Spain, [1993] ECR nyr, which refers extensively to article 128 with regards to cultural hindrances of the internal market.
68. Case 126/86, Giminez Zaera vs Instituto Nacional de la Seguridad Social and the Tesoria General de la Seguridad Social, [1987] ECR 3697.
69. See also the Council's answer to Written Question no. 2760/92 (Sotiris Kostopaulos) on AIDS in Greece, which refers to the 'Europe against AIDS' programme, OJ 1991, L 175. This programme may fall within the terms of article 129. However, the answer also refers to the supply of donor blood, which is an internal market issue, since provisions on it have been made in Dir. 89/381. This directive is based on article 100A.
70. See e.g. Morehead Dworkin, Steyger (1989), AIDS victims in the European Community and the United States, Are they protected from unjustified discrimination?, *Texas International Law Journal*, Vol. 24, no. 2, Spring.
71. Resolution of 13 November 1992 on monitoring and supervision of communicable diseases, OJ 1992, C 326/01.
72. Barents (1993), *supra* at 13.
73. See section II.2.
74. Case 45/86, Commission vs Council, [1987] ECR 1493; cases C-51/89, C-90/89 and C-94/89, United Kingdom vs Council, [1991] ECR I-2757.
75. Doc. SN 4482/92 of 11 November 1992.
76. See e.g. the judgments mentioned in note 34.
77. The reasoning of the Court that the member states acted effectively as trustees of the Community and the acting had no effect whatsoever on the division of powers must be kept in mind.
78. All these elements are to be found in the Conclusions of the Council in Edinburgh of 12 December 1992, Doc. SN/456/92, annex to part A, which, however, does not take any final stand on it.

IV Nailing the caskets

The directive as a device to define the relationship between the Community and its members

1 Introduction

The directive may be considered to be the most peculiar legislative device at the disposal of the Community. In no other international organization, nor in any existing federation, is a device with characteristics like the directive to be found.[1]

The directive is the legislative device most commonly used in the Community to achieve harmonization of laws. It is also used very often. Member states sometimes seem to be overwhelmed by the quantity (though not always by the quality) of directives which are showered upon them; sometimes they also give the impression of being totally surprised by the issues regulated in the directives concerned.

Since directives have to be transformed into national law, their enormous number causes serious problems for the member states. Often the transformation period prescribed in the directive is too short to allow the member states to follow the usual procedures in the legislative process. This is especially the case if the transformation of the directive requires the adoption of new statutory provisions. Even after thirty-six years of experience many member states still have not adjusted their complicated legislative processes to the requirements of transformation.[2] The case-law concerning this neglect has resulted in remarkable effects on the application of national law to situations regulated by a directive.

The main focus of this chapter will be on this impact of directives on the law of the member states. Therefore the consequences of the case-law concerning direct effect will be discussed from the viewpoint of the national administration. Over the years it has turned out, however, that directives have had an effect on national law well beyond the relevant laws meant to transform and implement the directive concerned. Already there is quite a lot of case-law of the Court of Justice which unexpectedly influences legal areas, such as civil and administrative law, which are at first sight unrelated to directives. This, what the author would call, 'second-generation' case-law will be discussed extensively. Furthermore, attention will be paid to the problems which the transformation of directives causes in national legal systems.

Before these areas can be explored, however, it is necessary to discuss the essentials of a directive. How are directives regulated in the Treaty and how are the powers between the Community and the member states divided where directives are concerned?

2 The essentials of directives

Though their name may be misleading, directives are legislative devices.

They usually intend to harmonize national law by prescribing to the member states the result to be achieved through transformation of the directive into national law. Member states are free to choose their own legal methods and the form in which to transform a directive. Member states can be held liable, however, if the desired result is not achieved.[3] The Court of Justice accepts very few defences from a member state if a directive is not properly transformed. The member state concerned cannot evade its responsibility by blaming decentralized governmental institutions,[4] national courts, or private individuals.[5]

While reading directives, the innocent reader will notice a striking resemblance to regulations. Directives often prescribe the result to be achieved with as much detail as the law laid down in regulations. And, just like directives, regulations instruct the member state to take certain measures for implementation. So the difference between regulations and directives does not seem so great. This appearance is deceptive. There is still a notable difference between these two forms of Community legislation.

As has already been said in chapter II, the power (and the obligation) to implement regulations derives from delegation. The power and the obligation to implement follow from the regulation itself, though the use of national law may be necessary to execute it. The Community may retain the power to implement regulations itself, if it wishes to do so. It is the Community legislator who decides how far the discretionary freedom to implement goes, not the member states.

The power to transform and implement directives, however, derives directly from the Treaty itself. Article 189 of the Treaty explicitly leaves the choice of form and method to the member states. This means that the member states are ultimately the ones who decide how a directive should be implemented, and not the Community legislator. Nevertheless, the Court has already limited the power of the member states to choose form and method considerably. On the question of how much detail a directive may go into when prescribing procedural requirements, the Court ruled in the ENKA judgment that the answer depends on whether the result to be achieved calls for such detail, in view of the specific nature of the field being regulated.[6] This view leaves room for the legislator to decide on an *ad hoc* basis the level of detail needed. Kapteyn c.s. argue that even in cases in which the field being regulated calls for it, a directive can never oblige a member state to introduce an exhaustive set of rules entirely unconnected with the national legislation in the context of which the field was regulated.[7]

Thus, the freedom to choose form and method is not absolute even though it is provided for by the Treaty itself. The Court has consistently regarded the adaption of administrative practices as a way to transform directives as a violation of Community law because of their unenforcable nature. According to the Court, directives should be transformed into legal provisions which can be relied on or enforced by individuals.[8] This case-law will be discussed more elaborately in section 3.1.

Another question is whether the Commission, as the main administrative body of the Community, is free to provide the member states with guidelines on transformation or implementation.[9] This question arose in the aftermath of discussions surrounding the Sutherland report.[10] The Commission proposed to issue such guidelines to ameliorate the transformation of Community legislation.[11] Since guidelines do not have a binding nature in itself, it may be argued that the Commission is entirely free to do so, because member states are entirely free to ignore them. Nevertheless, the present author would like to submit some doubts on the acceptability of Commission guidelines.

These doubts spring from the risk that the non-binding nature of guidelines might change into a quasi-legislative nature. This could happen if national Courts or the Court of Justice itself would take these guidelines into account in disputes concerning correct implementation. This is not an entirely theoretical suggestion. In the Netherlands as well as in other member states, policy rules, guidelines, and other quasi-legislative devices have evolved from opinions to rules having certain legal consequences.[12] Even the Court of Justice has held that non-binding measures such as resolutions and recommendations are not entirely without legal consequences even though they definitely are not directly applicable.[13]

Judges in general, as well as the Court itself, might be tempted to use such guidelines as a criterion to determine whether the disputed implementation of a directive has been correct. In such a case, a member state which implemented a directive in a way totally different from the method advised in the guidelines, might be implicitly required to prove that this different method also leads to the result prescribed by the directive. Such a burden of proof and the presumption following from the guidelines would be in itself incompatible with the freedom to choose form and method provided by the Treaty. So some caution should be advised on the introduction of non-binding guidelines.

The source of the power of the member states to transform and implement directives leads to an essential difference between regulations and directives. While the Court may consider itself empowered to interpret national law which is used to implement a regulation,[14] it is definitely not empowered to do so when it comes to the national law used to transform or implement directive provisions. Even when national law is explicitly adopted to transform a directive, the Court has no jurisdiction to interpret it. This law forms part of the national law and is susceptible to interpretation by the national courts only. As we saw in Chapter II, national law used for the implementation of regulations as such forms part of Community law.

Nevertheless, the case-law concerning the interpretation of directives has interfered considerably with the power of national judges to interpret national law. The differences between regulations and directives are in fact blurred by the case-law concerning the interpretation of national law by national judges if a question of Community law is involved. National statutory provisions can be examined to see whether they are within the framework of the directive. If these provisions are not consistent with that framework the national judge has to interpret the national law according to the directive ('concurrent' interpretation).[15] If this interpretation is not possible, the national judge may be required to suspend the application of the national provision.[16]

While interpreting directive provisions and imposing the obligation of a 'concurrent' interpretation of national law, legal principles included, the Court went as far as to accept an interpretative discretion which virtually alters national law on certain points. These judgments will be discussed below.

Another difference between regulations and directives is that directives do not have horizontal direct effect. While the Court of Justice accepted the direct effect in the relationship between government and individual,[17] it has never accepted that directives could confer obligations on individuals. Directives which are not transformed or are wrongly transformed into national law therefore have a very one-sided effect. They can be relied on against the government but not against other individuals.[18] Governments cannot impose sanctions on individuals for not complying with a directive which is not yet transformed;[19] they must also refrain from imposing sanctions on individuals complying with national law on the grounds that national law is incompatible with a directive.[20] Though the government may be obliged to apply a directive or a directive provision which has not been implemented directly, this does not remove the responsibility from the member state to compensate other individuals who have been treated disadvantageously because of this application.[21]

The fact that directives do not have a direct effect in procedures between individuals does not render them useless in these procedures. Since national law must be interpreted according to the result prescribed in directives, relying on a directive provision in a procedure between individuals can lead to a change in interpretation in the national law, so that the national law in fact becomes concurrent with the directive.[22] Also the declaration of a court, in a procedure between individuals, that the national law violates Community law, though it may not lead to an immediate victory for the claimant, may enable him to claim compensation against the state for the disadvantages caused by the non-implementation of the directive.

3 Directives in the case-law of the Court

The specific nature of directives has led to a wealth of case-law on questions such as direct effect and 'concurring' interpretation of national law. The doctrine of 'concurring' interpretation has given rise to many misgivings about the effects of directives; this case-law will be discussed below. Another question which is especially important for the member states is which government bodies are obliged to apply the directly effective provisions of a directive.

3.1 Direct application

The doctrine of direct effect when applied to directives is mostly regarded from the viewpoint of the individual invoking directive provisions against the government. The concept of direct effect finds, however, its mirror image in the obligation imposed on the government to apply directly effective directive provisions even though the directive has not yet been transformed into national law. This mirror image immediately addresses the question of to whom this obligation applies. In other words: which bodies must be considered as part of the government when it comes to the application of directive provisions.

In the series of judgments in which the Court first laid down its conditions for direct effect of directive provisions,[23] directives were invoked against the State as such. Since the State was the body which should have transformed the directive into national law, it appeared that the State could not invoke its own negligence against its citizens. This is not a doctrine unique for Community law; the doctrine of estoppel in international law derives from the same principle.[24] The Court repeatedly ruled in this sense.[25] This led some authors to conclude that direct effect of directive provisions was linked to the concept of negligence. directive provisions could only be invoked against member states which had been negligent. In the reverse this should have meant that only a negligent member state could be forced to apply directive provisions directly.[26] According to this theory, directives could not be directly invoked against other government bodies such as local or regional authorities, since these bodies had no part in transforming the directive.

The case-law of the Court proved this conclusion to be wrong. In cases concerning public procurement the Court started to extend the concept of 'government'. In Gebroeders Beentjes[27] the Court ruled that a local commission which as such did not belong to the local government, should be regarded as the local government whose decisions it replaced. This led to a revision in the Directive 71/305[28] on public procurement, in which the concept of government was extended so as to cover all kinds of public authorities. In other directives on public procurement as well as the directive codifying the three directives on public procurement, this extended concept was incorporated.

One could argue that the extension of the concept of government in the public procurement cases followed from the objective of the directives concerned. Obviously, these directives covered all public authorities, otherwise the objective of the directives would never be achieved. However, the Court also extended the concept of 'state' in other cases where it was not immediately apparent from the objective of the directive concerned. In Becker[29] the directive provision was not invoked against the state as such but against the tax authorities of the City of Münster. In Johnston[30] the claimant relied on a directive provision against a constitutionally independent body responsible for maintaining public order.

In Costanzo[31] the Court accepted that directive provisions could be invoked against local authorities. Though this last case was also a case concerning public procurement, the Court took a more general position than in the Gebroeders Beentjes judgment. While in Gebroeders Beentjes the Court related the application of the directive to the objective of the directive, in Costanzo it ruled that in general it would be an inherent contradiction to accept the view that individuals could rely on directive provisions against the government and still maintain that government institutions should not be required to apply these provisions because they could not be regarded as the (negligent) state as such. In other words, the requirement of negligence has vanished; government is government, whether it could implement a directive itself or not.

In Foster vs British Gas,[32] the Court went even further. In this sex-discrimination case, the question emerged whether Ms Foster and her companions could rely on a directive provision against a Gas Company once public but now privatized.[33] The Court confirmed this possibility by reasoning that

> '.... a body, whatever its legal form, which has been made responsible, pursuant to a measure adopted by the State, for providing a public service under the control of the State and has for that purpose special powers beyond those which result from the normal rules applicable in relations between individuals, is included in any event among the bodies against which the provisions of a directive capable of having direct effect may be relied upon.'

With the mirror-image of direct effect in mind, this judgment may lead to a certain confusion in the member states as to which bodies are obliged to apply directive provisions directly if the member state has failed to transform or failed to transform properly the provisions in national law. This is even more important because of the ruling in the Marshall judgment.[34] In this case the Court held that the question of whether a public authority acted as a public institution or as a private person (e.g. an employer) made no difference for the question of whether an individual could rely on directive provisions against them. In other words: if a public authority is obliged to apply directive provisions directly it has to do so while acting in all its capacities.

The question, then, is when exactly does a body fulfil the requirements of the Foster judgment. For example, when may a body be considered to provide a 'public service'? In fact: what is a 'public service'? According to the Court, it covers more than just the traditional functions of the state, like defense. For example, does health care fall within the concept of a 'public service'? Curtin submits that, at least in Britain, health care can not be regarded as a traditional public service because in Britain the state only assumed responsibility for it in 1946.[35] Nevertheless, the Court ruled in Marshall that British health care authorities should apply directive provisions directly. Should broadcasting be regarded as a 'public service'? Though there definitely will be some latitude for the member states to determine whether an activity is a 'public service' depending on the traditions in the member states themselves, in the last instance the Court shall have to define the limits of what may be regarded as such with regard to the application of Community law.

Even more difficult may be the concept of 'control of the State'. Does this mean that the body should have to be established by statutory provisions or that its tasks are determined by statutory provisions? Or is it enough that bodies are licenced or financed by the State? After all, states can in fact control bodies just by attaching conditions to licences or by limiting funds.

For example, in the Netherlands public broadcasting is being provided by subsidized, licenced but, nevertheless, private institutions. Do they belong to the institutions who have to apply directly applicable directive provisions?[36] In the Netherlands, the same question can be asked for health care. The mixture of subsidies, licences, and legislation which provides the State with a certain measure of control over the institutions providing health care is chaotic and difficult to untie. To determine whether this health care system falls within the scope of the Foster judgment is by no means an easy task. This means it is not clear whether these institutions should apply directive provisions directly. It has to be hoped that future case-law from the Court will resolve these uncertainties.

3.2 *Case-law of the second generation: directives as a means to transform national law*

Since it was first adopted, the doctrine of 'concurrent' interpretation in relation to directives has led to a wealth of case-law on the way national judges have to interpret national law. While the first cases dealt with direct discrepancies between national legislation implementing directives and Community law,[37] by now a kind of 'second generation' case-law has emerged which affects general concepts in the constitutional, administrative, and civil law of the member states.

Though 'concurrent' interpretation does not require changes in national law as such, the changes required in interpretation of the national law are sometimes so profound that one could say the doctrine of compliant interpretation is virtually transforming the national legal landscape. By enforcing the doctrine, the Court wove a net of implicit obligations which the member states will have to adhere to while implementing Community law. The cases discussed in this section mostly deal with the implementation of directives. However, the doctrine of 'concurrent' intepretation applies to Community law in general as well as to directives. Thus, some of the quoted cases, though relevant for the interpretation of directives, may also concern Treaty provisions.

The implicit obligations imposed by the Court not only affect the interpretation of national legislation but also of national legal principles. Because directives have to be implemented in national law, they are meant to form part of the national law. This means that other concepts in national law like national legal principles might create exceptions in situations covered by the provisions of a directive. The result could be that the obligation prescribed in the directive may have different results in different member states.

Such a basic principle of national law was set aside in Cotter and McDermott vs Minister for Social Welfare and Attorney General II.[38] In their first case, concerning social security, Ms Cotter and Ms McDermott had relied on Directive 79/9[39] (equal treatment of men and women in statutory social security) against their Government. In that case the Court of Justice ruled that the Irish unemployment benefits were discriminating because they supplied married men with higher benefits than married women. Married men automatically received supplementary benefits for dependent spouses and children, while married women only received these supplementary benefits if they could prove they were the breadwinners. While the case was pending before the Court, Cotter and McDermott brought new proceedings before the Court, seeking, *inter alia*, a declaration that they were entitled to the same increases in their social security benefits as married men in the same circumstances received during the disputed period (there was a change in the legislation during the proceedings).

Those new proceedings and the follow-up of their earlier proceedings were heard together before the national (High) court. This allowed their application only in part, rejecting in particular their claims with respect to increases for adult and child dependents. The national court considered that it would be unfair and inequitable to pay those sums to the applicants when their spouses were not dependent on them. On appeal and in the proceedings before the Court of Justice, the respondents argued that to allow these claims would go against the principle of unjust enrichment, a basic principle of equity.

Though in earlier cases[40] member states had successfully invoked the national principle of unjust enrichment before the Court, in this case the Court dismissed the principle in one simple sentence. It ruled that 'to permit reliance on that prohibition would enable the national authorities to use their own unlawful conduct as a ground for depriving article 4(1) of the directive of its full effect.' So the national judge must not allow basic principles of law to interfere with the application of Community law, once Community law is clearly violated.

Because directives are implemented in national law, national civil or administrative procedures are applicable to the actions to enforce directive obligations. The Court of Justice ruled that procedural conditions which intend to ensure the protection of the rights of individuals and which derive from the direct effect of Community Law, should not be less favourable than those relating to similar actions of a domestic nature, nor framed so as to render virtually impossible the excercise of rights conferred by Community law.[41] This interpretation of procedural law also affects the time limits set for bringing proceedings. As long as a directive is not properly implemented, Community law precludes the competent authorities of member states, in proceedings brought against them by an individual, from relying on national procedural rules relating to time limits for bringing proceedings.[42] The Court is not going so far as to preclude the government from relying on other kinds of time limits. Time limits necessary for the proper administration of, for example, social security law may be invoked against the individual, even though the member state did not comply with its duty to implement the directive timely.[43]

In Johnston vs Royal Ulster Constabulary[44] the right to a remedy against discrimination was at stake. The case dealt with discriminatory treatment of female police officers in the RUC, because they were not allowed to carry weapons. Ms Johnston complained before the Industrial Tribunal of Northern Ireland and relied on both the Sex Discrimination Order 1976 and Directive 76/207. In the proceedings before the Tribunal the Chief Constable produced a certificate issued by the Secretary of State in which, according to article 53 of the Sex Discrimination order, was stated that the treatment of Ms Johnston was done for the purpose of 'a. safeguarding national security and b. protecting public safety and public order.' Article 52(1) of the Sex Discrimination Order provides that none of its provisions prohibiting discrimination '... shall render unlawful an act done for the purpose of safeguarding national security or of protecting public safety or public order'. In addition, article 53(2) provides that a certificate signed by or on behalf of the Secretary of State certifying that an act was done for the purpose mentioned in article 53(1) was conclusive evidence that it was done for that purpose.

These provisions would have had the effect of depriving Ms Johnson of every remedy. Because she also relied on the Equal Treatment Directive, the Industrial Tribunal referred the case to the Court of Justice for a preliminary ruling on the issue.

The Court held that it followed from article 6 of the directive that member states must take measures which are sufficiently effective to achieve the aim of the directive and that they must ensure that the rights thus conferred may be effectively relied upon before national courts. The member states are under a duty to ensure effective judicial control as regards compliance with the applicable provisions of Community law. They are also under a duty to ensure the compatibility with Community law of national legislation intended to effect the rights for which the directive provides. A provision like article 53(3) of the Sex Discrimination Order is contrary to this principle of effective judicial control, because the certificate as mentioned in this article deprives an individual of the ability to assert the rights conferred by the directive by judicial process.

In Heylens[45] the Court extended this rule and imposed the obligation to provide for an effective remedy in every case in which the national authority denies individuals rights which are provided for by the Treaty. The obligation of the State to provide for a remedy is extended to cover situtations in which it leaves certain decisions to public enterprises.[46]

In Factortame vs Secretary of State for Transport[47] the Court required another procedural guarantee for the protection of rights conferred by directives. The case dealt with a ruling of the English Court of Appeal concerning the 1988 Registration Law for fishing vessels. The Court of Appeal suspended the law during a preliminary procedure before the Court of Justice. The Secretary of State appealed against the suspension on the grounds that no such provisional measure exists under English law. After preliminary questions asked by the House of Lords, the Court ruled that to ensure the protection of rights conferred by the Community, national courts have the obligation to take the necessary provisional measures in order to ensure the full effect of Community law, even if they are not allowed to do so under national law.

The procedural rules concerning the burden of proof in civil law have also been under judicial review. According to the Court these rules have to be interpreted in conformity with certain rules, at least when it comes to the application of the Equal Treatment Directives. In Danfoss[48] the Court ruled that the employer is required to prove non-discriminatory conduct in cases in which discriminatory conduct is alleged. To become eligible for such a reversal of the burden of proof, the allegations of discriminatory conduct must be based on objective factors such as statistics showing that more women than men in the same situation are disadvantaged.[49]

The implicit obligations conferred by directives do not only affect procedural requirements. Sometimes long existing national civil law may also be affected. In Von Colson and Kamann vs Land Nordrhein-Westfalen[50] and Harz vs Deutsche Tradax[51] the statutory compensation of the German Civil Code in sex discrimination cases came under attack. The Civil Code provided only for compensation for the loss incurred by candidates who are victims of discriminatory practices in establishing an employment relationship.

The Court of Justice held that the requirements to interpret their national law in the light and the wording of the directive (in this case the Equal Treatment Directive 76/207) led to the non-applicability of these provisions of the Civil Code. It ruled that 'it (was) impossible to establish real equality of opportunity without an appropriate system of sanctions'. Even though sanctions are within the jurisdiction of the member state, they have to be in conformity with community law.

In Dekker vs Stichting Vormingscentrum voor Jong Volwassenen[52] the Court ruled that the national concept of negligence in a tort procedure was not applicable when it comes to application of Community law. The case dealt with an application procedure for a job from which a pregnant woman was excluded. In the Netherlands the only remedy against discrimination in job application is the tort procedure. To establish whether an act must be regarded as unlawful, there are five requirements. One of these requirements is that the party acting unlawfully should have acted with a certain measure of negligence. Although member states are free to determine the remedies to enforce the directive, the Court of Justice held that these remedies cannot result in additional requirements before the tort is established. In other words, the breach of Community law is enough to establish the tort, any other requirements of national law should not be applied in case of violation of Community law.

In Marleasing[53] the Court required the national judge not to apply a provision in Spanish civil law. The case dealt with the question of whether a company could be declared null and void for reasons to be found in Spanish law only. Because of the limited list of justifiable reasons to declare companies null and void incorporated in Directive 68/151,[54] the Spanish judge was not allowed to issue such a declaration on any other grounds than those listed in the directive. The existing provision in the Spanish Civil Code, which actually provided for other grounds, could thus not be applied, even though the fact that the judge could not apply these provisions could be regarded as a violation of the principle of legal security against the party demanding the declaration. It has been argued that in this judgment the Court exceeded the limits of what 'concurrent' interpretation can do.[55] While directives in themselves cannot impose obligations (or more specific disadvantages) on individuals, the result of the ruling of the Court in this case was exactly that.

The most far-reaching effect of 'concurrent' interpretation may be found in the Francovich judgment.[56] The judgment concerned the neglect of Italy to implement Directive 80/987.[57] Directive 89/987 obliged the member state to adopt provisions for the organization, financing, and effectuation of funds by employers, which would compensate their employees for the losses or part of the losses incurred by the insolvency of the employer. Italy had not transformed the directive into national law, so the insolvency funds had not been established. While the directive provision in itself could not be directly applicable, Andrea Francovich and Daniela Bonifaci sued the Italian Republic for the loss incurred by the failure to implement the directive. The Court ruled that the full effect of Community law could not be achieved if individuals who had incurred losses because of the neglect of the State could not be compensated by the negligent state itself, especially in cases where the direct application of directive provision was not feasible.[58] It ruled that the State should be held liable in cases where the directive provision concerned conferred rights on the individual, those rights were clearly determined in the provision itself, and the losses incurred by the individual were caused by the neglect of the State to implement the directive.

The key words in the case-law concerning the implicit obligations of the member states are 'full effect'. National judges interpreting national legislation have to ensure this 'full effect' by conforming the national provisions as much as possible to Community law. Though the application of the doctrine by the Court in itself does not intend to change the national legislation, in practice it does. If the application of a national statute, principle, or procedural requirement threatens to deprive a directive (or Community law in general) of its full effect, the national court is not allowed to apply it. Hence the national judge has to interpret national law differently when the issue is covered by Community law than when it is covered by national law only. In some cases the national legislator may even be obliged to abolish the provision as far as the implementation of a directive is concerned. On the other hand, if the national law omits a requirement to ensure full effect, the national judge has to invent one and apply it.

This means, in general, that the application of national law, even when that law was never meant to be harmonized or even affected by Community law, needs to be adapted to ensure the full effect of Community law. Judges applying their national laws and statutory requirements according to national traditions and implicit or explicit legal principles often have to change their application and interpretation in the light of one all-embracing Community legal principle: the principle of full effect of Community law.

It is not clear how tight this embrace of the principle of full effect may eventually become. In the Netherlands some confusion over its boundaries in civil procedures has already emerged. By now even leading principles of civil law, such as the passive attitude of judges in determining the extent of disputes have been questioned.

Article 48 of the Dutch Code on Civil Procedures provides for the passivity of the judges. Dutch civil judges are not allowed to take account of facts not supplied by the applicants. The content as well as the extent of the dispute submitted to the court is determined by the disputing parties only. Judges are only allowed to correct deficiencies in the legal basis of a claim; they are not allowed to base their judgment on other facts than those submitted by the parties. This is the case even when the facts submitted are clearly insufficient to provide the disputing parties with a balanced judgment and other facts are well known to the judge.

Therefore, whether Community law can be applied or whether preliminary questions can be asked may depend on the facts submitted by the parties in a civil procedure. If the facts submitted do not sustain the (probable) application of Community law, the national judge cannot apply it in a procedure.

The following example may illustrate this: sexual harassment as such is not yet clearly included as discriminatory conduct in Directive 76/207 on equal treatment of men and women. If a woman claims compensation from an employer because she is sexually harassed, but she does not claim she is discriminated against, if she does not explicitly rely on the directive concerned, and if all the facts she submits points unambiguously to harassment only and not to discrimination, the national judge is not allowed to base its judgment on anything other than harassment. He is therefore not enabled to ask preliminary questions on the application of Directive 76/207 because the facts do not sustain the claim of its applicability. Depending on the phrasing of the case, he might only be able to ask the question of whether the directive covers sexual harassment as such. Only if this answer is affirmative may he ask questions concerning the interpretation and application of the directive.[59]

Though this has been accepted for many years, according to Ter Kuile Community law abolishes this restriction on the Courts. He feels the full observance of Community law may entail an obligation for the national judge to rely on facts not submitted in the procedure, and thereby to exceed the dispute as submitted by the plaintiff and defendant, in order to secure the full effect of Community law.[60] He submits that the application of Community law does not belong to the realm of national law but to the realm of Community law. Therefore national legal restrictions such as those mentioned above, should not apply when they frustrate the full effect of Community law. Others, however, defend the freedom of the parties to define and to determine the extent of their disputes.[61]

Recently, preliminary questions concerning this restriction of the powers of national judges have been posed to the Court of Justice. In a Dutch case concerning the compulsory association with an occupational pension scheme for physiotherapists the appellant claimed, in appeal before the Supreme Court (cassation), that the courts below should have applied articles 3(f), 5, 85 and 90 of the Treaty, even though these articles were not relied on, and no facts sustaining their applicability were submitted in the original case.[62] Since Dutch law obliges the Supreme Court to restrict itself to reviewing the proper application of the law and it is not allowed to review the facts, it could only declare that according to Dutch law the judges are not allowed to examine the applicability of the above mentioned Treaty articles because of the lack of relevant facts in the original case. It could not itself examine the applicability, because it is not allowed to review the facts at all.

The Supreme Court conceded, however, that the question whether lower courts should have been obliged to apply the Treaty article concerned could be a question of Community law. In a preliminary procedure before the Court of Justice, it asked the Court of Justice whether the national court is obliged to apply Community law, even though the application should require it to base its final judgments on facts not supplied by any of the parties to the proceedings.[63] A second question concerned the disputed obligation of the Supreme Court to examine the above mentioned facts if and when the facts are only submitted in the highest resort, even while national law explicitly prevents the Supreme Court from examining the facts of submitted cases in civil procedures.

This author expects the Court of Justice to answer these questions in the negative.[64] If the Court would rule that judges are obliged to exceed the boundaries of the dispute submitted by a plaintiff and defendant just to ensure the full effect of Community law, the result would be that the plaintiffs' reasons for confining their claims to certain facts would be ignored. Thus, the application of the doctrine of 'concurrent' interpretation would essentially mean that the full effect of Community law becomes more important than the rights of individuals bringing their claims to court. Such an interpretation eventually would not only transform national law, but would violate one of the most important legal principles in a democratic country: the freedom of the individual to determine what he wishes to dispute in a civil procedure.

4 Problems of transformation

According to article 189 of the Treaty, the result of directives is binding, while member states choose form and method to achieve the result in their national legal system. In effect this means directives have to be transformed into national law.

Directives usually provide for a certain period to achieve this transformation. As we have already seen, the moment of expiration of the transformation period is the moment the government of a state may become obliged to apply the directive directly. The transformation periods incorporated in directives vary from some six months for simple directives (such as Commission directives elaborating on details) up to some six years for complicated directives and directives regulating politically sensitive areas.[65] The average transformation period is somewhere between eighteen months and two years.

Although the transformation periods seem to be quite long, frequently member states are not able to transform their national law in time. This has to do with various factors, some of which are more acceptable than others. Member states often claim the time needed for adoption of legislative provisions prevents them from transforming in time. Since Community law as such does not affect national constitutional law, member states have to adopt legislation according to the usual constitutional procedures. This means that if a directive requires the adoption of a new statute, the parliamentary procedures, as well as mandatory advisory procedures have to be adhered to. The fact that the legislation is necessary on the grounds of the obligations to transform a directive is not an excuse to circumvent those (in themselves democratic) procedures.[66] In such a case there may be delays, especially if the national parliament objects to the new law, while the government no longer has any freedom of choice because of the detailed nature or the clarity of the directive provisions. Such problems could of course be prevented by improving the parliamentary information and consulting procedures about directives. Then the national parliament could voice its objections during an earlier stage, such as the process of adoption of the directive itself.

Another problem member states face is that national governments often give insufficient priority to the transformation of directives. In so far as politicians are more interested in conducting their own national policies (policies which might improve their chances to be re-elected) transformation of directives must compete for resources with other legislative and policy-making activities that are regarded as more urgent and more important.[67]

The process of transformation into national law may also suffer from different meanings attached to concepts used in national law and Community law, which may lead to different interpretations in the two legal systems. These differences could slow down the actual transformation considerably.

A more fundamental problem often mentioned by member states is that the traditional way to deal with a certain subject is not by issuing regulations in the sense of legislative or administrative provisions, but by regulating through more quasi-legislative methods like codes of practices or self-binding guidelines of the administration. Sometimes the regulation of subjects is entirely left to society itself through self-regulatory devices such as collective agreements. Since these traditional methods are often rooted in the traditional ways of dealing with certain policy areas, they are sometimes hard to replace by formal rules determined by the state. In the following section the author intends to explore these problems by reviewing the case-law of the Court concerning the options for the member states with regard to the form and methods for implementation.

4.1 Transformation into national law

Directives have to be transformed into national law. What is meant by 'law' may differ from one country to another. For example, in some member states law solely derived from case-law without any incorporation in statutory provisions is more common than in others; in such cases case-law may more often lead to changes in legislation. The Court of Justice does not concern itself with those kind of differences. It implicitly accepted implementation of a directive through consistent case-law of the national courts, even though the judgments the case-law consisted of went directly against the words of the law concerned.[68] If case-law is not considered that important in the member state concerned, it simply is not the problem of the Court.

Transformation of directives into national law usually means transformation into directly enforcable law. Unless the directive itself leaves room for other forms and methods than directly enforcable legal devices,[69] one has to assume that a transformation into law which can be relied on and enforced by individuals is necessary. If existing legislation already implements the directive, explicit transformation is of course superfluous.[70]

This insistence on the adoption of directly enforcable provisions means that transformation into national law through simply changing the practice of the administration is not sufficient, because those practices can be changed at will and are not always generally known or widely published.[71]

According to Heukels[72] it is doubtful whether administative practices which are widely known will suffice as a means to transform. In a case on the directive concerning the profession of general nurses, the Court ruled that a generally known and irreversible administrative practice covered by general principles of law did not suffice. It considered those (in themselves binding) general principles not specific enough to ensure the observance of the very detailed provisions of the directive concerned.[73]

Published guidelines instructing the administration on how to use its administrative powers have not been approved as means sufficient for transformation. In themselves no real difference exists between administrative practices and published guidelines.[74] Both are meant to bind the administration in its dealing with individuals, so as to serve certain principles of proper administration such as equality and the prohibition of arbitrariness. The difference might be that published guidelines are more widely known and therefore may be easier for individuals to rely on.

In a case concerning a German published guideline, the *Technische Anleitung zur Reinhaltung der Luft*, the Court ruled that if the directive aims to ensure the rights of individuals, such guidelines are not sufficient to transform the directive into national law.[75] The fact that the guideline concerned was based on a statutory provision and, according to the German government, the administration could not depart from the guideline even in atypical cases did not make any difference. According to the Court, guidelines do not suffice because they leave individuals without knowledge of the full extent of their rights and obligations.[76]

In these last cases the Court itself distinguishes between directive provisions intending to protect the rights of individuals and other provisions where the transformation into national law by published guidelines is concerned. This may lead to the conclusion that published guidelines may be used to implement directive provisions other than the ones intended to protect the rights of individuals. One may think of instructions for the administration on the application of definitions in national legislation which are less detailed than the definitions used in directives. Depending on the room the national legislation leaves for such a change, a published guideline could be used to broaden or narrow a definition in national legislation. Especially in the case of existing legislation such a guideline for the administration may accelerate the transformation process. And since judges interpreting such provisions are already obliged to interpret in conformity with directive provisions, instructions in the form of published guidelines to the administration executing the legislation concerned may really be helpful in accelerating the transformation process.

Transformation into national law which is not promulgated by the

State has also provided the Court with problems. Self-regulation of society has not been accepted nor embraced fully by the Community institutions. Nevertheless, the desire in certain member states to leave certain issues to be regulated by society rather than the State must be faced by the Community in the future.[77] In fact, problems concerning self-regulatory measures already emerged in the social field, and have led to a series of judgments by the Court.

In some member states, the government hardly interferes with some areas of the law, such as collective bargaining in industrial relations. In Denmark, for example, labour contracts and major parts of labour law are governed exclusively through collective agreements.[78] This absence of government interference may become a problem when the Community issues directives to regulate certain parts of labour relations. The adoption of the equal remuneration and equal treatment directives already led to such mandatory interference by the government. Currently directives are being discussed which require an even further interference by the national governments on other labour conditions such as working hours.

Whether these kind of self-regulatory devices are acceptable as method for the transformation of directives depends primarily on the status of such devices in national law. Only if self-regulatory devices are enforcable by the contracting parties as well as by the individuals covered by them can they be considered as a sufficient method of implementation according to the Court. In Great Britain, for example, collective agreements are not enforcable in court; one has to assume British collective agreements do not suffice as a means for transformation.[79]

While achieving the prescribed result of directives is a responsibility of the member states, under certain conditions the Court of Justice has accepted self-regulatory measures as a means for the transformation of directives. The first recognition that an area covered by Community law might be dealt with through self-regulatory measures came quite implicitly. In a case concerning the registration of domestic physicians the Court accepted the referral of an arbitration tribunal to the Court, thereby acknowledging the fact that the obligation derived from Community law was transformed into national law through regulations of a professional organization.[80] Nevertheless, in its judgment the Court explicitly emphasized that the member state had left the Community obligation in the care of such a professional organization, thereby implying that this could be seen as a proper way to transform the directive concerned.

In later judgments the Court more explicitly accepted the possibility of self-regulation as a proper form for transforming directives into national law. In case 91/81,[81] concerning the transformation of the directive on collective dismissals in Italy, the Court to some extent accepted the argument of Italy that the directive had been implemented through collective agreements. It ruled that Italy had failed to fulfil its obligations only with regard to the matters not covered by collective agreements. In a case against Denmark[82] concerning the transformation of the Equal Pay Directive, the Court expressed its position on self-regulatory measures more clearly. It ruled that: 'member states may leave the implementation of the principle of equal pay in the first instance to representatives of management and labour'. However, if an effective protection is not ensured by those means and, in particular, there are no collective agreements, or the existing ones do not cover all workers, the member states are required to adopt legislative or administrative provisions. The same approach was followed in a case[83] concerning the transformation of the directive on transfers of undertakings.[84]

These judgments imply self-regulatory measures such as legally binding agreements may be acceptable provided that they ensure full compliance with all the obligations imposed on the member states by the directive. The Court even accepted a collective agreement as a means of implementation of the Collective Dismissals Directive, when its scope had been extended *erga omnes* through the use of a legal instrument.[85]

This case-law indicates there is room for the implementation of directives through self-regulatory devices. At least in the social field and the field of professional organizations the Court has already accepted self-regulation under certain conditions as a means of transformation. There is no reason to expect it would be different where codes of practice are drawn up by representative private bodies, for example to regulate advertising. Nevertheless, the State remains responsible for the transformation and has to intervene if the regulating organization or the bargaining parties do not achieve the desired result.

In view of the responsibility of the member states, in most cases there will be a need for some legislation to ensure the fulfilment of all obligations. At least the possibility of quick government intervention has to be provided for.

The Court has consistently interpreted the terms 'form and method' in the light of the responsibility of the member state and in the light of the abilities of individuals to enforce rights granted by directives. This interpretation has led to the acceptance of enforcable agreements and consistent national case-law, as well as legislative provisions on all levels, as suitable means of transformation, but virtually left out administrative measures other than legislation.

This easier acceptance of collective agreements compared to administrative measures may follow from the fact that collective agreements are traditionally more accepted and have a more similar appearance in most

European countries. Although differences exist between the member states, collective agreements appear throughout Europe as enforcable contracts covering large groups of workers. These agreements are most often located within an extensive system of contractual rules. Only Great Britain proves to be the exception.

This cannot be said of administrative practices and guidelines. The ability of individuals to rely on administrative practices and published guidelines differs from state to state, and it often differs according to the status of the guideline or practice concerned in national law. To distinguish the different legal consequences of administrative practices and published guidelines by itself would probably be too much for the Court.[86]

The question of what may be accepted as being 'law' in the sense of 'law sufficient to transform a directive' is answered by the Court alone. This means that, when it comes to the transformation of directives, doctrines in the member states themselves on what should be regarded as 'law' are less relevant then they are in the national legal systems.

Since directives should be transformed into national law and are thus subsumed into the national legal order one may question the justifiability of the requirements the Court imposes on the concept of 'law'.[87] If a member state views and applies published guidelines as 'law',[88] and enables individuals to rely on them, should not the member state itself determine whether these guidelines are appropriate to be used as a device for transformation? Is it appropriate that a Court declares it to be a violation of Community law if these devices are being used, while it clearly does not have the resources to examine these devices extensively? But maybe the existing case-law of the Court is not yet the end of the story.

What has been submitted above applies even more to transformation through self-regulatory measures. Community law is starting to affect areas which have not been subject to state control until now, but traditionally have been left to the self-regulatory capacity of society. If the Community desires to add those areas to the jurisdiction of the Community, it might be forced to use more and more of the legal traditions of the societies it wants to control in order to achieve the desired result. State legislation might prove to be less effective than the self-regulatory capacity of the societies within those states. It may be the greatest challenge in Community legislative circles to explore ways to fit those national self-regulatory traditions into Community law.

4.1.1 The use of concepts in national and Community law. Another problem which emerges while transforming directives into national law are the different meanings of legal concepts used in the different legal texts. The different meanings of concepts are not a feature which emerges exclusively where directives are concerned. The texts of the Treaty and regulations also contain terms and concepts which have meanings which differ from the meaning they have in national law. For example the concept of 'worker' in article 48 of the Treaty does not mean entirely the same as the term 'worker' or 'employee' in Dutch law.[89]

The different meanings attached to concepts to be found in Treaty provisions or regulations do not pose a problem in most cases, however, since only the Court of Justice eventually determines the meaning of these concepts. If it comes to the interpretation of concepts derived from directives, the situation may, however, be different.

Since the transformation of directives into national law actually makes them a part of national law, usually concepts used in national law are applied to the transformed directives. For example, directives concerned with the protection of workers protect those working people who are 'workers' as determined by national law.[90] Only concepts which are vital for the full effect of the directive are interpreted by the Court.[91] If concepts are not considered vital, differences between the member states may exist.

Thus member states which have properly transformed a directive, may nevertheless face a judgment of the Court ruling that they are violating Community law, because of a different interpretation of a concept used in a directive. The problem for the member states is that there is no clear doctrine on which concepts must be considered vital. Actually, the case-law on the subject is quite underdeveloped, so for the member states it remains a gamble whether they should use their national concepts or invent new ones the interpretation of which, if need be, can be adapted to the interpretation the Court provides for the same concept in the directive concerned. This may become a problem if the member state has defined the concept explicitly in its national law.

This problem could be avoided if the Community legislator itself would define the concepts it considers vital for the full effect in the directives concerned. This has not always been done so far.

5 Defining the relationship between Europe and its members; some concluding remarks

Since the establishment of the Community, the directive has been the most ambivalent device in the structure of Community law. Originally meant to impose obligations on member states while respecting the legal traditions of the member states, directives have developed into devices which actually interfere quite strongly with those traditions.

The original intent concerning directives and their effects followed from the Treaty provisions, which laid down a fairly traditional focus on the EC-organization as it was then. The Community developed, however, from an international organization in which the member states joined, to a kind of pre-federal government which directly affects the daily lives of individuals.

In the case-law of the Court of Justice, directives have led to a definition of 'government' which may very well differ from the view on what can be seen as 'government' by the member states. It has also imposed obligations on the member states concerning the interpretation of the law only remotely related to Community law in general, and often even more remotely related to the directives which have to be transformed. Finally the Court has defined what should be considered 'law' if it comes to the transformation of directives.

In a federal state this kind of intrusion is to be expected. Though in a federation powers are still left to the smaller units (states, Länder), it follows logically from the concept of a federation that the federal Constitution defines such concepts as 'legal principles', 'government', and what may be considered 'law' in general, logically follows from the concept of a federation. One may even assume that the members of a federal state explicitly opted for such unity.

In an organization such as the Community this may be viewed differently. The Treaty explicitly left alone the constitutional legal order and the internal organization of the member states including the legal concepts belonging to it. With regard to directives this power of the member states to incorporate directives into the national law as it sees fit is even stipulated in the Treaty establishing the EEC. So the redefining by the Court of national concepts such as 'law' does not seem so logical at all. But, over the years, Community law developed in such a fashion nevertheless.

So it may be submitted that the development of Community law concerning directives is a development towards a federation, albeit implicitly. Nowhere has the Court of Justice even suggested that outside the Community jurisdiction member states should define concepts as 'government', 'law', 'legal principles' or 'legal devices' in the way member states are obliged to do inside the Community jurisdiction. Nevertheless, member states have to reckon with these requirements of Community law, almost every time a new law is being made. This is the case even if the newly regulated area belongs entirely to the jurisdiction of the member state. Even law laid down in directives remotely related to the objectives and means of the Treaty generates this effect. The result may be that national concepts may become harmonized without any Community interference, but only as a result of the case-law concerning the requirements of Community law in general and of directives in particular.

The above-cited case-law therefore at least leads to the conclusion that directives by now can be seen as devices used within a federal context. Though according to the wording of the Treaty, directives are not intended to affect the constitutional legal order of the member states, in practice they do exactly that. In the relation with regulations this means that though directives differ in method to achieve federal jurisdiction, as an ultimate result the differences have vanished.

Notes

1. Kapteyn, VerLoren van Themaat, Gormley (1989), *Introduction to the Law of the European Communities*, Kluwer, Deventer, 193.
2. The Dutch government has only recently started the discussion on shortened legislative procedures after being urged by the Commissie voor de Toetsing van Wetgevingsprojecten (The Committee on review of legislative projects). See the Cabinet position paper *Voortvarend wetgeven*, TK 1993/94, 23 462, nr. 1.
3. E.g. Case 300/81, Commission vs Italian Republic, [1983] ECR 449.
4. Cases 96/81 and 97/81, Commission vs The Netherlands, [1982] ECR 1791, 1819.
5. Case 80/86, Kolpinghuis, [1987] ECR 3969.
6. Case 38/77, ENKA BV vs Inspecteur der Invoerrechten en Accijnzen, [1977] ECR 2203.
7. Kapteyn, VerLoren van Themaat, Gormley, *supra* at 196.
8. Case 97/81, Commission vs The Netherlands, [1982] ECR 1819; case 429/85, Commission vs Italy, [1988] ECR 843; case C-339/87, Commission vs The Netherlands, [1990] ECR I-851.
9. Transformation means the formal subsumption of Directives into national law; implementation means the actual effectuation of the substance of a Directive.
10. High Level Group on the Operation of the Internal Market (1992), *The Internal Market after 1992, Meeting the Challenge* (Sutherland Report), CEC Brussels.
11. Doc. SEC(92) 2277 final, recommendation 37.
12. Ganz (1987), *Quasi-legislation; Recent Developments in Secondary Legislation*, Sweet & Maxwell, London; Van Kreveld (1983), *Beleidsregels in het recht*, Kluwer, Deventer; Van der Meulen, Steyger c.s. (1991), Bestuurs-

bevoegdheid als bron van recht, *Nederlands Tijdschrift voor Bestuursrecht*, 133-141.
13. Case 59/75, Manghera, [1976] ECR 91 (on resolutions).
14. See section II.3.2.
15. Case 80/86, Kolpinghuis Nijmegen BV, [1987] ECR 3969.
16. Cases 51/76, VNO, [1977] ECR 113; 38/77, Enka, [1977] ECR 2203.
17. Case 41/74, Yvonne Van Duyn vs Home Office, [1974] ECR 1337.
18. Case 152/84, Marshall vs Southampton and South West Health Authority, [1986] ECR 723; case C-91/92, Paola Faccini Dori, 14 July 1994, [1994] ECR nyr.
19. Case 148/78, Publicco Ministero vs Ratti, [1979] ECR 1629.
20. Case 80/86, Kolpinghuis, [1987] ECR 3969.
21. Steyger (1993), Nogmaals over 177 EG, aalscholvers en pursers, *Nederlands Juristenblad*, 1482-1483.
22. According to some authors 'concurrent' interpretation is a method to sneak in horizontal direct effect of Directives, e.g. Keus (1993), Europees privaatrecht, een bonte lappendeken, in *Preadviezen voor de vereniging voor Burgerlijk recht en de Nederlandse vereniging voor Europees recht*, Koninklijke Vermande, Lelystad, 58.
23. The provision has to be unconditional and sufficiently precise, as well as not leaving any real discretion as to the result to be achieved (case 41/74, [1974] ECR 1337, see also case 71/85, FNV vs The Netherlands, [1986] ECR 3855). Also the transformation period must have expired (case 148/78, Ratti, [1979] ECR 1629).
24. Prechal (1990), Remedies after Marshall, *Common Market Law Review*, Summer.
25. Case 148/78, *supra*; case 8/81, Becker vs Finanzamt Münster Innenstadt, [1983] ECR 53; case C-91/92, Paola Faccini Dori vs Recreb Srl., 14 July 1994, [1994] ECR nyr.
26. Lauwaars, Maarleveld (1987), *Harmonisatie van wetgeving in Europese organisaties*, Kluwer, Deventer, 68, 69.
27. Case 31/87, Gebroeders Beentjes, [1988] ECR 4635.
28. Dir. 71/305, JO 1971 L 185, on public procurement of works. It was revised in the way described through Dir. 89/440, OJ 1989 L 210.
29. Case 8/81, *supra*.
30. Case 222/84, Johnston vs Royal Ulster Constabulary, [1986] ECR 1651.
31. Case 103/88, Fratelli Constanzo vs Commune di Milano, [1989] ECR 1839.
32. Case C-188/89, Foster vs British Gas Plc, [1990] ECR I-3313.
33. On the details of the case see e.g. Steyger (1991), De directe toepassing van richtlijnen door anderen dan de Staat, *RegelMaat* no. 1, 10-13.
34. Case 152/84, Marshall vs Southampton and South West Hampshire Health Authority, [1986] ECR 723.
35. Curtin (1990), The province of government, delimiting the direct effect of directives in the common law context, *European Law Review*, 215.
36. According to the conclusion of A-G Tesauro in case C-148/91, Dutch

broadcasting institutions should be regarded as such; the Court left this question unanswered (case 148/91, Vereniging Veronica Omroep Organisatie vs Commissariaat voor de Media, 3 February 1993, [1993] ECR nyr).

37. Case 51/76, Verbond van Nederlandse Ondernemingen vs Inspecteur der Invoerrechten en Accijnzen, [1977] ECR 113; case 38/77, ENKA vs Inspecteur der Invoerrechten en Accijnzen, [1977] ECR 2203; also case 80/86, Kolpinghuis Nijmegen BV, [1987] ECR 3969.
38. Case C-377/89, [1991] ECR I-5357. See *supra* note 5, see *infra* text.
39. Case 61/79, Amministrazione delle Finanze della Stato vs Denkavit Italiana Srl., [1980] ECR 1205.
40. Case 68/79, Hans Just vs Danish Ministry for Fiscal Affairs, [1980] ECR 501.
41. Case 33/76, Rewe Zentralfinanz and Rewe Zentral AG vs Landwirtschaftskammer für das Saarland, [1976] ECR 1989; Case 199/82, Amministrazione delle Finanze dello Stato vs San Georgio SpA, [1983] ECR 3595.
42. Case C-208/90, Theresa Emmott vs the minister for Social Welfare and the Attorney General, [1991] ECR I-4269.
43. Case C-338/91, Steenhorst-Neerings, 27 October 1993, [1993] ECR nyr.
44. Case 222/84, [1986] ECR 1651.
45. Case 222/86, Heylens, [1987] ECR 4097.
46. Cases C-46/90 and C-93/91, J.-M. Lagauche, 27 October 1993, [1993] ECR nyr.
47. Case C-213/89, [1990] ECR 2433.
48. Case 109/88, Danfoss, [1989] ECR 3199.
49. Also case C-127/92, P.M. Enderby vs Frenchay Health Authority (FHA), 27 October 1993, [1993] ECR nyr.
50. Case 14/83, [1984] ECR 1891.
51. Case 79/83, [1984] ECR 1921.
52. Case C-177/88, [1990] ECR I-3941.
53. Case C-106/89, Marleasing, [1990] ECR I-4135.
54. JO 1968 L 65/8.
55. Keus (1993), *supra* at 60-62; otherwise, Prechal (1991), Richtlijnconforme uitleg, Alice in Wonderland, *Weekblad voor Fiscaal Recht*, 1991/5984, 1596 and Timmermans in *SEW* 1992, 816.
56. Cases C-6/90 and C-9/90, Andrea Francovich and Daniela Bonifaci vs Italian Republic, [1991] ECR I-5357.
57. Dir. 89/987, OJ 1980 L 283, concerning the protection of workers in case of the insolvency of the employer.
58. The Francovich-judgment immediately led to two other preliminary questions concerning the scope of the obligation to compensate in case of neglect, see joined cases C-46/93, Brasserie du pêcheur SA vs Federal Republic of Germany and C-48/93, Factortame III, both pending.
59. See e.g. case C-13/94, P. vs S. and Cornwall County Council, pending, concerning the question whether Dir. 76/207 covers a dismissal on the grounds of transsexuality.
60. Ter Kuile (1993), Het verband tussen artikel 177 EG, aalscholvers en

pursers, *Nederlands Juristenblad*, 1136-1141.

61. Mok (1993), Over aalscholvers en bijscholing van rechters, *Nederlands Juristenblad*, 1244-1245; Verbraeken (1993), Dicatuur van het gemeenschapsrecht, *Nederlands Juristenblad*, 1483-1484.
62. Van Schijndel vs Pensioenfonds voor Fysiotherapeuten, HR 22 oktober 1993, *Rechtspraak van de Week* 1993, no. 210.
63. Case C-430/93, Van Schijndel vs Pensioenfonds voor Fysiotherapeuten, pending.
64. See e.g. case C-348/89, Menacarte-Metalurgica da Lagao Lda. vs Chefe do Serviço da Conferencia Final da Alfandega do Porto, [1991] ECR I-3277 in which the Court stresses the autonomy of the individual judge to determine if and when preliminary questions should be asked if a question concerning national law is disputed at the same time. See also the Dutch intervention in joined cases C-340/93 and C-341/93.
65. E.g. Directive 86/368 on equal treatment of men and women in occupational pension schemes. The transformation period of the law expired in 1992, the transformation period of the schemes concerned expires in 1995.
66. In some member states special statutes providing for delegation of regulatory power exclusively to transform Directives in national law have been adopted, see e.g. Mortelmans (1982), Delegatiewetten ter uitvoering van verdragen en met name ter uitvoering van verplichtingen opgelegd door het Europese Gemeenschapsrecht, in *Liber Amicorum J. Mertens de Wilmars*, Kluwer, Antwerpen, 135.
67. Bekkers, Bonnes, De Moor-van Vugt, Voermans (1993), *Brussel en Nederland, tegenliggers, spookrijders of reisgenoten, Implementatie van EG-regelingen in de Nederlandse rechtsorde*, Schoordijk Instituut, W.E.J. Tjeenk Willink, Zwolle, 145-189.
68. The national judges consistently interpreted a discriminatory statutory provision as violating article 26 of the Convention on Civil and Political Rights thereby in fact replacing the discriminatory provision: case C-338/91, Steenhorst-Neerings, [1993] ECR nyr.
69. Such an exception is to be found in Dir. 85/339, OJ 1985 L 176 (transformation through voluntary agreements); see also Heukels (1993), Alternatieve implementatietechnieken en art. 189 lid 3 EEG; grondslagen en ontwikkelingen, *Nederlands Tijdschrift voor Bestuursrecht* 93/1, 61-62.
70. Case 29/84, Commission vs Germany, [1985] ECR 1661; case 22/87, Commission vs Italy, [1989] ECR 143.
71. See the case-law mentioned in note 6 *supra*.
72. Heukels (1993), *supra* at 66.
73. Case 29/84, Commission vs Germany, [1985] ECR 1661.
74. The Court did not differentiate between published and non-published administrative practices in case 239/85, Commission vs Belgium, [1986] ECR 3645.
75. Cases C-361/88, Commission vs Germany, [1991] ECR I-2567 and C-58/89, Commission vs Germany, [1991] ECR I-2607.
76. See also cases C-13/90, C-14/90 and C-64/90, Commission vs France,

[1991] ECR nyr.

77. Steyger (1993), European Community Law and the Self-regulatory Capacity of Society, *Journal of Common Market Studies*, Volume 31 no. 2, June, 171-190.
78. Nilsen (1987), *Learebog i arbejdsret*, Kopenhagen.
79. Legal service of the Council, 23 November 1984, doc 10550/84 IUR 148 SOC 323; also Lord Wedderburn (1986), *The Worker and the Law*, Penguin Books, Harmondsworth, 303; Steyger (1990), *Medezeggenschap bij veiligheid en gezondheid: de Europese regelingen*, Kluwer, Deventer, 79.
80. Case 246/80, C. Broekmeulen vs Huisartsen registratie commissie, [1981] ECR 2311. In an earlier case the Court accepted that the regulation of a private social security fund might be seen as the implementation of a regulation; see case 61/65, Weduwe Vaassen vs Bestuur Beambtenfonds Mijnbedrijf, [1965] ECR 257.
81. Case 91/81, Commission vs Italy, [1982] ECR 2133.
82. Case 143/83, Commission vs Denmark, [1985] ECR 427.
83. Case 235/84, Commission vs Italy, [1986] ECR 2291.
84. The official name of the Directive is: Directive on the protection of workers in case of transfer of undertakings.
85. Case 215/83, Commission vs Belgium, [1985] ECR 1039.
86. The Court itself did not just accept the arguments of the German government but verified them in TA-Luft (case C-59/89, Commission vs Germany, [1991] ECR I-2607).
87. See also Steyger (1993), JCMSt, *supra* at 183.
88. In the Netherlands, for example, not only the government, but even the Supreme Court under certain circumstances regards published guidelines as 'law' to be applied by the courts; see HR 28 March 1990, NJ 1991, 119 (Guidelines on administrative fines); HR 29 June 1990, NJ 1991, 120 (Guidelines on immigration); see also Van der Meulen, Steyger c.s. (1991), *supra* at 133-141.
89. Case 53/81, Levin, [1982] ECR 1035; case 139/85, Kempf, [1986] ECR 1741.
90. Case 19/83, Wendelboe, [1985] ECR 457; case 105/84, Mikkelsen vs Danmols, [1985] ECR 2639.
91. For example case C-29/91, Sophie Redmond Stichting vs H. Bartol, 19 May 1992, [1992] ECR nyr (on the concept of undertaking in Directive 77/187); case 227/82, Van Bennekom, [1983] ECR 3883 (on the concept of pharmaceutical specialty in Dir. 65/65); case C-369/88, Delattre, [1991] ECR 1487 (on the concept of disease in Dir. 65/65).

V Destiny unknown

Some concluding remarks

1 Introduction

In the preceding chapters the relationship between the Community and its members has been analyzed from a legal point of view. It turned out that the legal orders of the Community and its members, though constitutionally still separate, are intertwined in various ways.

The Community's ability to delegate regulatory powers to the member states already points to a certain subordination of the member states toward the Community. The concepts of direct effect, which can lead to the inapplicability of national legal provisions, and supremacy, which imposes the obligation on national judges to interpret the national law in a way prescribed by the Court, reinforce this subordination. Developed in the case-law of the Court, these concepts definitely bind the members to the Community and lead to a greater loss of independence and sovereignty than was probably anticipated when concluding the original Treaty establishing the EEC.

Also, the addition of more and more policy areas, whether through the influence of the internal market or though incorporation in the Treaty, implies an (often unintended) continuing intertwining development. The incorporation of the principle of subsidiarity may be characterized as the clearest acknowledgement of the growing subordination of the member states to the Community. Subsidiarity is only necessary, then, when a development of centralization is feared. Such a development is feared only when the members acknowledge the supremacy of the central administrative level. To determine at which level powers should be used, a substantive criterion is needed. And to determine the level at which to use powers, the powers disputed should be available for use on all the levels.

Finally, the development of the applicability of directives is really startling. Orginally intended as a device which would leave it to the member states to achieve a certain harmonizing result in their own ways, it developed into a device through which the Community could not only achieve harmonization of the issue regulated by the directive, but through which it could have an impact on general concepts of law.

Many of these developments are due to the judgments of the Court of Justice. The Court gave the Community the upper hand, often to the astonishment of the member states. Nevertheless, in many issues the member states accepted their role in a federal state, though often grudgingly.

Facing these developments, which definitely leave the member states with a loss of sovereign power, one might ponder the question posed in the first Chapter. Has a state been constituted by now? May one consider the Community a federation yet, or is it becoming one in the near future?

To answer this question it is necessary to examine the legal elements constituting the relationship between the Communty and its members with regard to their federal potential. But to prevent giving undue weight to the legal point of view, it is also necessary to ask: what is in fact needed to constitute a (federal) state, and do the necessary ingredients exist in Europe?

2 The legal point of view: Europe and its members

From a legal point of view there are several elements in the relationship between the Community and its members which definitely have a federal character. As we saw in Chapter I, some of these elements were already incorporated into the Treaty in the fifties, so the question of whether the Community was ever intended to be a federal state or not is not as far-fetched and revolutionary as some of the Eurosceptics (a new brand of politicians, who by 1993 started noticing an integration process which already existed for quite a while) may feel.

With regard to external relations, the Community has been provided with the power to conclude treaties with third countries. This power is limited to the subjects covered by the Treaty. On some subjects the Community is exclusively empowered to conclude these treaties, the Commission being its only representative, on others the Community and the member states have concurring powers. To confer the power to determine the external relationships on often important subjects which affect individuals certainly is a federal feature of Community law. If one takes into account that on many areas which do not belong to the jurisdiction of the Community at all, the member states try to co-ordinate their point of view within the European Union, one might at least say that the external relations field is a promising field for growth towards a federal state.

Internally, the relationship between the Community and its members acquired most of its federal character through the case-law of the Court of Justice. Though the foundations for the steady extension of the powers of the Community were laid in the Treaty itself, for example in article 177, which grants the Court the exclusive power to interpret Community law, it is the way the Court has built on those foundations which must be seen as vital in this respect. As early as 1964, in the judgments Van Gend en Loos[1] and Costa-ENEL,[2] the Court adopted the doctrines of direct effect and supremacy of Community law, which constituted a revolution in itself. These judgments positioned the legal order of the Community as a separate entity. The legal orders of the member states were subordinated to the legal order of the Community as far as the application and implementation of Community law was concerned.

Furthermore, the case-law concerning the application of human rights in Community law has led to an interpretation which could only be achieved in a federation. National measures should not violate human rights, as interpreted by the Court, if these measures are somehow covered by Community law.[3]

The way the Court 'tamed' the national judges when it came to their application of Commmunity law also contributed to the federal character of Community law. The Court not only required the member states to comply with its judgments, but it also required the national judges to comply with Community law in general, and directives in particular. This is even the case when there is no judgment of the Court to comply with in a particular case. This case-law caused directives to evolve from a legal device not too different from legal devices in other international organizations to a legislative device which virtually resembles national legislation.[4]

The case-law concerning the interpretation of vital concepts in the Treaty has added its own dynamics to the development of a more federal Community. As far as free movement within the Community was concerned, the concepts of goods, workers, establishment and services were interpreted broadly and apparently without regard for the limits originally intended. This considerably extended the policy areas which the Community could regulate. And, as we saw in Chapter II, these extensions in turn led to further extensions.

The extension of the jurisdiction of the Community to certain policy areas, solely on the strength of the general concept of the internal market and without explicit consent of the member states, is also a feature not uncommon to federal states. Though federal constitutions usually explicitly divide the powers between the federation and the states, the states most often have to accept an interpretation of that division in favour of the federation. Apparently the wish for unification of the law in the federation prevails over the wish of the states to regulate according to their own traditions.[5]

This development of extending the powers of the federation is not always consistent and may sometimes be stalled temporarily, depending on the political situation in the federation. The development in the Community is not unique in that respect. In the United States as well as in the Community, a retreat of the powers of the federation in favour of those of the (member) states can be seen at the moment. In the United States this development is to be seen mainly in relation to sensitive issues such as the question whether the Constitutional right of privacy prevents the state from adopting measures restricting abortion.[6] In the Community the clearest example of this trend is to be found in the recent judgment Keck and Mithouard[7] in which the Court explicitly overturned earlier case-law, thereby restoring to the member states the power to adopt certain non-discriminatory measures which might potentially and indirectly hinder the free movement of goods.

The retreat of federal judges is often inspired by political developments and dilemmas which cannot be solved by law (federal or domestic) alone. Though the developments in the United States are largely due to an increase in the number of conservative judges on the Supreme Court, a heritage of the Reagan and Bush administrations, it may also result from a certain enmity to the strong influence of federal law in the recent past.[8] In the Community the retreat of the Court may also have more than one reason. The aversion in the European countries to the ongoing European integration, culminating in the not too favourable referenda on the Treaty of Maastricht in Denmark and France, may have caused the Court to slam on the brakes for a while. More down to earth, the retreat may also be due to a desire to reduce the increasing caseload of the Court, caused by lawyers invoking Community law in every case concerning national measures which might be remotely related to the four freedoms.[9]

In spite of these developments, the federal elements already incorporated in the original Treaty most certainly were strengthened through the development of the legal order of the Community. It is the Court which is calling the shots when it comes to this development, even though for a long time no sanctions whatsoever existed against judgments violating the rulings of the Court. But even that has changed. In Francovich[10] the Court held member states liable for violating Community law; since national judges form part of the member state, there is no reason why the Francovich judgment should not apply to rulings violating Community law, especially when these rulings are contrary to explicit judgments of the Court. Moreover, even the member states recognize the desirability of sanctions, to be imposed on member states who repeatedly ignore judgments of the Court; so the possibility of a fine for repeated violations of Community law was incorporated in the Treaty of Maastricht.[11]

By imposing the concepts of direct applicability and supremacy of Community law with their consequences for the national legal order of the member states, the Court established Community law as being supreme, just as in the United States the federal law is regarded as the 'supreme law of the land'. When it comes to the internal relations between the Community and its members, at least from the legal point of view the Community has got virtually all of the characteristics of a federation. The mere fact that the constitutional legal order of the members in itself is not affected, and that the members retain the power to organize large parts of their internal affairs, does not affect this view. The extent of these powers is determined by Community law, in so far as Community law covers the internal affairs to be regulated. And, even more importantly, the member states can only marginally influence the extension of the areas covered by Community law and therefore only marginally influence the extent of the limits imposed by Community law.

Of course differences still exist between acknowledged federations such as the United States and the Community. In the field of external relations, the powers the Community possesses are still very limited when compared with those attributed to the federal government of the United States. Also, hardly any powers of the Community exist in the field of criminal justice. The question whether criminal laws should be harmonized is hotly disputed and no concept of federal crime exists in the Community.[12] Also the Community has no jurisdiction over the immigration laws of the member states as far as subjects of third countries are concerned. Some member states agreed to open their borders under the Agreement of Schengen, but this agreement has been concluded separately from the Community and is not ratified by all member states. However, this could easily change. Already, the open borders between some of the member states have led to grave problems with regard to organized crime and the number of asylum seekers, causing the Dutch Secretary of State for Justice to propose an immigration policy at the European level.[13]

But from the legal point of view, the Community already is, or is fast becoming, a federal entity; the question of whether it is or could become a federal state depends on many more factors than the law alone.

3 What constitutes a 'state'?

To determine whether an entity could become a 'State', whether federal or not, is quite a difficult excercise. The concept of a 'State' as such is easy to define, as it is largely a legal concept. With legal criteria, derived from international as well from national law, one may determine what kind of entity acts like most of the states we acknowledge as such. Lawyers, like me, tend to be satisfied with those criteria and to ignore all others while drawing conclusions.

But legal criteria most often describe only part of the reality people live in. The legal concept of a 'State' as such says little about the way it is generally perceived by its inhabitants. Therefore something more is needed, which, for want of a better word, is probably best described as a 'nation'. Though historically not synonymous, over the years the notions 'state' and 'nation' have become strongly attached to each other in the sense that a 'state' which is not a 'nation' is quite a fragile construction.[14] Contemporary history shows this. Entities acknowledged as and generally perceived as states, and for us Western Europeans as nations too, like the Soviet Union, Czechoslovakia and most of all Yugoslavia, fell apart the moment the political conditions within those entities changed. For their inhabitants, these entities apparently were not perceived as nations after all, but only as states.

So to determine whether the Community, or the European Union if you like, has some viability as a state, one should determine whether the Community has some of the characteristics of a nation. The criteria for what constitutes a 'nation' are less clear than the criteria for what constitutes a state: legal characteristics simply are not enough. Whether an entity might be viable as a nation depends on historical, sociological, geographical and cultural factors. To determine whether the Community is a (federal) state in all respects, or is likely to become one in the not too distant future, these factors have to be taken into account.

To be sure, the present author does not pretend to offer an overall theory on the elements necessary to constitute a nation. The only aim is to review a few of the existing differences between the member states and compare them with the same factors in acknowledged nations, in order to examine whether they might or might not prevent the Community from ever becoming one.

3.1 'Them' and 'us': the Europeans as a people

To us, twentieth-century citizens, 'states', 'nations' and 'peoples' are inextricably linked. Though, to some extent it is acknowledged that a state can be inhabited by different peoples, the general feeling by now is that state and people are, if not synonymous, at least related in the sense that a state or a nation without a 'people' is not a very viable concept. The existence and special status of 'peoples' is recognized in international law too; the right of self-determination of peoples has been laid down in several treaties and resolutions of the United Nations[15] and is acknowledged by the International Court of Justice.[16] Though it is not imperative that excercising this right should lead to the establishment of a state, it is usually invoked against oppression by another people who form the dominating group in an existing state. The result of the quest for self-determination is sometimes the establishment of a separate state, but just as often more oppression or civil war.

The logical question, then, is: what is a people? What characteristics does a group of persons need to proclaim itself a 'people'? To define 'people' may be even more difficult than to define 'nation'. One may think of characteristics such as ethnic origins, a common language, a common culture, a common religion, but the moment one lists these determinants, there are groups defining themselves as a people, or which are defined as a people by others, which do not fit these determinants at all.

The most striking example is, of course, the 'Jewish people'. There is hardly any common ground between Jews over the world, except for religion (and even within the concept of 'Jewish people' there are non-religious Jews) and maybe some remnants of a shared culture. But practically all other common factors have vanished through some two-thousand years of diaspora.[17] Nevertheless, one speaks about the 'Jewish people' as if it were a people like any other. Also, many people of Jewish descent, even if they are not religious, have a sense of belonging to a Jewish 'people', even though the sense of belonging sometimes can be attributed more to the actions of non-Jews than to their own beliefs[18].

Another example can be found in the United States. Regardless of origins, religion and often even language, most citizens of the United States define themselves as Americans, whether they are interested in their background or not. Nobody would ever claim that the descendants of the British, the Africans, the Irish, the Polish, the Asians, the Russians, the Italians or the Mexicans (to name some of the main ethnic groups) inhabiting the United States started out as one people. Nevertheless, at least the second generation of immigrants, and often the first, refer to themselves as belonging to the American people, if not towards fellow-Americans, at least towards citizens of other countries.

Maybe that is what it all comes down to: the feeling of an 'us' as opposed to a 'them'. This is not to say that the above-mentioned factors are irrelevant; on the contrary, it is just that the feeling of 'us' and 'them' added to one of these or any other factors is one of the preconditions to be able to consider oneself a 'people'.

If the presupposition that 'state' and 'people' are related is correct, and a state without a 'people' is hard to imagine or is at least a quite fragile construction, the question is whether the concept of 'people' applies or could apply to the group of citizens of the member states living in the territory of the Community. Legally these citizens are already citizens of the European Union. The Treaty of Maastricht establishes this citizenship,[19] and endows the citizens with some rights such as the right to move and reside freely within the territory of the member states, the right to vote and to be elected in municipal elections and in elections for the European Parliament in the member state of residence. Also, the citizens of the Union are entitled to protection by the diplomatic consular authories of any member state in third countries in which their own member state is not represented.

So, legally we are Europeans after all. But do we feel like Europeans? Do we have a common feeling as Europeans, that is a common feeling of 'us'? In certain circumstances we definitely have. Those of us who travel or have travelled the shores of the Mediterranean in their twenties, often do remember a distinct feeling of being an European. Nationality does not count that much when you meet lots of contemporaries, with whom you solve the world's problems while sipping gallons of cheap wine in nice tavernas, with whom you fall in love and with whom you sleep on the beaches. Feeling European that way is definitely great, but does it last? And is it enough to constitute a people?

With regard to 'us' in opposition to 'them' an example of European behaviour came when the Iranian government condemned the writer Salman Rushdie to death because of the contents of his novel 'The Satanic Verses'. The outcry that this was not the way things are done over here came not only from the European governments but also from many people in countries all over Europe. And 'here' was Europe, not just Great Britain, 'we' were Europeans, 'they' were the others.

But these are the exceptions: in most cases 'us' is used while referring to one's own nationality. Things happening in other member states do not affect 'us' as much as they affect 'them'. For example, for people in

Holland the Troubles in Northern Ireland have always been a very distant thing; it affected 'us' only when it came to our doorstep with some terrorist actions in the city of Roermond. Nevertheless, these Troubles constituted a small civil war, being fought right within the Community.

Whether there ever will be a European 'us' is completely unpredictable. The chance that the different peoples will learn to know each other better has grown, however, due to the greater opportunities for traveling, and to extended oppportunities to visit schools and universities in other member states. This increasing knowledge of each other can lead to a better understanding which might diminish the classifications as 'them' of other European peoples, even if it does not immediately lead to a classification as 'us' of one European people. And maybe it is possible to establish a European federal state with a score of peoples tied together by the absence of 'them' in relation to each other, rather than a common feeling of 'us'.

In the author's opinion that would not be such a bad result. The classifications of 'us' and 'them' are generalizations, which may easily lead to the discrimination of individuals. Whether positive (Greeks are so friendly, Germans are so thorough) or negative (Italians are so disorganized, the Danes are so boring),[20] generalizations are seldom true and never apply to the individual. Nevertheless, the conduct of every individual is likely to be judged according to the general characterizations of his background, including his nationality. And judging according to generalizations is one of the essential elements of discrimination, in fact it is the element hardest to eliminate. So if the European peoples could reach a stage in which they do not regard each other as 'them' and do not hold too many generalizing views of each other anymore (I am not so optimistic as to expect that we can eliminate them all), we really could achieve a European Union somewhat more civilized than we have now.

3.2 *History, culture and language*

Three other elements, often associated with the 'state' in the sense of nation, are its history, its language and its culture. One argument often heard from Eurosceptics is that the absence of any common history, culture or language prevents the Community from ever becoming a state.

One can say that, on the face of it, the establishment of existing Western European states was only achieved after a long, somehow shared history of the inhabitants of the eventual territory of the state. Within their current borders the development of the existing member states towards their current form started from some two- or three-thousand years ago for some, for others it can be traced to much later dates, depending on the view one takes. If one takes these long histories into account, it is arguable that the Community as such has no such shared history at all; it was established as a predominantly legal and economical construction only after the Second World War.

But in this author's opinion that view is too narrow. Of course the existent states have at least some specific history related to the region in which the state was originally established. Otherwise they would probably never have become separate entities at all. But to separate these regional histories from the entire history of Europe, as if these regions, which later came to be national states, did not derive that status exactly from their surroundings, would be ridiculous. The mere fact that national states are what they are now has everything to do with the collective history of Europe.

States came into existence mostly because of wars and bloodshed in Europe, wars caused by religious differences, by ethnic enmity, by the desire for power and sometimes by sheer madness. Alliances were formed and were broken up, often resulting in the establishment or disappearance of states. Can the current borders of Austria really be explained without recalling the history of the First World War and its alliance with Germany beforehand? Can the existence of the separate states of the Netherlands and Belgium be understood without reviewing the roles of Spain and the Habsburg dynasty in the sixteenth century? Is the history of Ireland really one which can be read without mentioning the British rule?

Asking these questions is providing the answer at the same time. Europe shares a common history in many respects, even though different regions, states, nations, and people were involved in different ways and at different times. Also that common involvement is not a very nice one, it consisted mainly of wars and bloodshed. The fact that this common history is largely ignored in favour of the specific history of the states is at least partly due to the interpretations which the evolving states attached to that history. In a state like the Netherlands, the eighty years' war with Spain which brought the Netherlands into existence as a state is regarded as one of the main events in history. For the Spanish it was just a slight uprising somewhere on the fringes of their gigantic empire.

One may argue that, though a common European history exists, a common history of the Community definitely does not exist. This is undoubtedly true, but what else is new? The establishment of the Community followed the most bloody war in Europe (and the world) ever, in which the most heinous crimes were committed. Something had to be done to prevent that from ever happening again. In this light the establishment of the Community as an organization integrating the different states economically, with the potential to evolve into a federal state eventually, does not seem that weird historically. Maybe the novelty was that the founding fathers did not want to achieve that federal state through oppression of the people inhabiting it.

There is of course a relationship between history and culture. One might argue that even if one accepts the notion of a common history of Europe, it has not led to a common culture, because it is a history of continuing enmity between states, peoples and regions. This absence of a common European culture is used as another argument against the Community eventually becoming a federal state. The differences in cultural identity between the member states would be too huge to ever melt into one and the same.

One may wonder if that view is entirely correct. On the face of it one would say yes. The differences between the member states, emerging in virtually every aspect of life, are undeniably great. To remain in my own limited field: even in the legal culture the differences between the Northern and the Southern member states[21] are immense. In the North the law is taken seriously; though we acknowledge that the flesh is sometimes weaker than it should be, there is a general feeling that laws should be adhered to and that laws should be written in such a way that it is possible to adhere to them. In the South the law is foremost one of the many rules and habits of life; coming in handy when and if needed, but adapted to practice when necessary.

A most striking example of the differences between those cultures could be watched in the fall of 1990. When the Belgian Parliament adopted a law to legalize abortion the then King of the Belgians, Bauduin, a declared opponent of abortion, could not in good conscience sign that law. His signature, however, was needed to formalize the law. The King acknowledged that to refrain from signing would offend his people as well the principle of democracy in Belgium, but the neat constitutional solution, abdication of the King, was generally regarded as undesirable. The creative solution of the Belgian government was found in the Constitution itself. The Belgian Constitution contains an article which enables the government to step in, if and when the King is unable to perform his royal duties. This article is generally perceived to be written to continue the governing process in case a reigning king suddenly gets very ill, has a stroke, goes mad, or something like that. In this case, it was applied to King Bauduin, who, with his consent, was declared to be unable to perform his royal functions for the period needed to formalize the law. The Belgian people generally thought it an excellent solution. The Dutch, whose constitution contains a similar article, were appalled. Though they understood the dilemma, among lawyers there was a general feeling this was not the way law should be used.

So differences between the member states definitely do exist. But does this prove a total absence of a common European culture? One may argue that those differences are so visible to everyone precisely because underneath these differences lies a set of values more or less common to all (Western) European nations (and to other nations like the United States as well). It is not to say that these values are very clear or equally applied throughout Europe. But certain liberal values like a somewhat measurable respect for the individual, his beliefs, his feelings, values partly embodied in the European Convention on the Protection of Human Rights, may be part of a common European cultural heritage, a heritage in which Europe differs from regions on other continents. The differences between the member states may seem so profound to us, precisely because they evolved from those common values. And maybe that is why so many European countries feel so devastated in periods of total disregard of these values, for example during the Third Reich or during the government of the Greek Junta.

So to achieve a certain common European culture in the here and now, maybe we should build on those common values, maybe we should strive to reconstruct them from our common past.

This is all nice and well, I can hear you think, but a reconstruction like that may take ages and the Community has to deal with those undeniable cultural differences right now. How to construct a nation on those differences, especially when the member states value their own cultural identity deeply? My answer would be the following.

Firstly, to construct a nation to achieve a state, it is not necessary that those cultural differences should vanish completely. The existing states within the Community contain some cultural differences in themselves. It has not kept them from becoming nations. The United States may be an even clearer example. The cultural differences which exist over there do not only spring from the origins or race of the inhabitants. Regional differences exist too, even if the main culture derives from Anglo-Saxon origins. The differences between, for example, places like Chicago and Philadelpha (not to mention New York) are striking, and the innocent traveller experiences them immediately after arrival. And those two places are not that far apart and have grown out of the same industrial roots. The differences between North and South in the United States are well-known. Being a woman in Texas is something entirely different from being a woman in New England.

In fact the regional differences in the United States are so profound that, in the early eighties, it caused Washington Post editor Joel Garreau[22] to speculate whether North America was falling apart into nine different nations, each characterized by its own main sources of income and therefore its own interests, but also its own cultural identity. Though these cultural differences definitely did not vanish, thirteen years later his prophesies have not yet materialized and do not seem about to do so in the near future.

So maybe it is possible for a nation to adapt to all those different cultures. Of course there is a difference between a nation possibly falling apart and one trying to come into existence, but do not be fooled by America's current size and number of states. The coming into existence of the United States as it is now was quite a slow process of adding newly acquired territories to the Union, and the Americans needed a civil war to keep it together. That federation has a history too. Of course negotiating with newly inhabited areas (of course these areas were not that newly inhabited, but who asked the natives) is different from negotiating with long existing states, as in Europe. But before it has been tried, one cannot say one cannot do it only for reasons of history and culture. Too many examples of successful federal movements exist.

Directly related to the cultural identity of the member states is the issue of language. The number of languages in Europe is really a problem for an effective integration. There are simply too many. The number of official languages of the Community was already up to nine. A tenth (Irish) is recognized by the Court as an official language of a member state,[23] even though it is not used within the Community. With the recnt growth to fifteen members, the Community will find itself a state with eleven official languages.

This number is already causing a lot of practical troubles, such as problems with the translations of documents within the Community. It may cause even bigger problems for the growth of a nation. In itself, for a nation to have one (main) language is not imperative. Many exist while having more than one. Switzerland has four, without apparently causing any trouble. Twelve might be overdoing it, though.

Inhabitants of a nation with eleven languages simply cannot master them all. Two or three besides one's mother tongue might be feasible, but eleven, no.

The language problem is at least partly caused by the member states emphasizing their language as a part of their cultural identity. For while throughout history language as such was not always the most prominent feature of states or nations, the current states often promoted one (sometimes two) dominant language, thereby repressing dialects or other languages spoken within the state. This emphasis on a national language prevents the member states from arriving at the only logical solution: the elevation of two or three of the official languages to a kind of lingua franca within the Community.

Since every measure to diminish the number of languages in the Community would cause an uproar, the Community itself is maybe wisest by not even trying it. It could be a problem which solves itself. Contrary to popular feeling, established languages are not eternal; they tend to change, to adapt and sometimes even to disappear over the years. Maybe the solution presents itself if one realizes that the use of too many languages is too costly and economically disadvantageous.

4 Destiny unknown

When the Community started in the fifties, nobody could have predicted its destiny. It could have been one of those initiatives which stranded after a few years, well-intended but not really grounded in reality. Sometimes during its history it looked like it would end like that: in 1966 when France practically opted out, in the late seventies, when nobody seemed to hear anything of the Community anymore. When one reads the newspapers, it seems that even these days the Community is far from safe.

It must be said that one of the causes of these swinging moods towards the Community has to do with public relations. The Community is not very good at those. In the past the Community was best known for its butter mountains and its wine lakes, and its trail of trucks travelling between Stassbourg, Luxembourg and Brussels, delivering the crates of the European Parliament. Nowadays we watch the quite ridiculous negotiations between the member states over the power to stop certain legislative proposals and developments in the Community, resulting in such horrors as the Protocol on Social Policy attached to the Treaty of Maastricht, and the deadlocks which sometimes occur in the negotiations with aspiring members. The Community has been ridiculed for these things, but apparently it never felt compelled to explain them.

And this nearly exclusively bad publicity is so unnecessary in the light of what is achieved. The Community has not been some kind of fancy action programme only to disappear in obscurity a few years after its establishment. Thanks to the Court of Justice and its consistently federal approach of Community law and the efforts of the Community legislator, Europeans are practically citizens of a federal state, whether they feel like it or not. The freedoms of trade, work and travel within the Community and so many more achievements in so many fields have definitely been worth the trouble. The problem is, however, that the Europeans do not attribute these attainments to the Community at all. Moreover, they do not understand the character of the Community, have no idea how it works and what influence it has on our daily lives. And this kind of ignorance often leads to resentment.

In this author's opinion it is of high importance that the Community makes more clear than ever what it does and why, to what it is empowered and what is left to the member states. To be governed by a virtually unknown entity, somewhere out there in 'Brussels' is irritating and maybe even frightening. If the Community wants to control its destiny somewhat more, more explanations should be a first step.

What this destiny will be is as yet unknown. One has to admire our travellers, starting with six, now up to fifteen and in the future even more. They started out on their expedition blind, never knowing where it would end and how it would end. Despite their difficulties they stayed together and maybe in the end that is the most important achievement of all.

Notes

1. Case 26/62, [1963] ECR 1.
2. Case 6/64, [1964] ECR 585.
3. See section II.2.1.2.
4. Case C-106/89, Marleasing, [1990] ECR I-4135.
5. For the development in the United States see Tribe (1988), *American Constitutional Law*, Mineola, New York.
6. Webster v. Reproductive Health Services, 109 S. Ct 3040 (1989); Planned Parenthood of Pennsylvania et al. v. Roberts P. Casey et al., S. Ct 1992 WL 142546 (U.S.).
7. Joined cases C-267/91 and C-268/91, [1993] ECR nyr.
8. See also Tribe (1992), *Abortion, the Clash of Absolutes*, Norton and Company, New York, 191.
9. The increasing case load has already led to problems in providing the member states with translations of the cases within a reasonable time; to avoid problems in this respect, since 1 January 1994 the Court delivers translations of the reports on the case only in the original language of the procedure.
10. Cases C-6/90 and C-9/90, [1991] ECR I-5357.
11. The rephrased article 171 provides for the possibility of the Court to impose a lump sum or a penalty payment after the member state has repeatedly ignored a judgment of the Court and the time period for complying imposed by the Commission has expired.
12. See e.g. Vervaele (1994), *Handen en tanden van het Gemeenschapsrecht, beschouwingen over publieke rechtshandhaving*, Kluwer, Deventer.
13. NRC-Handelsblad, 21 March 1994, Opinion of the Editor.

14. The close relationship between nation and state is most clearly expressed in the Irish national anthem entitled 'A nation once again' while it in fact celebrates the (re)establishment of a state. Though 'long a province' it never ceased to be a nation.
15. E.g. Articles 1 and 55 of the Charter of the United Nations; Article 1 of the International Treaty on Civil and Political Rights, 19 December 1979; Res. 637a (VII) of 16 December 1952, Res.1514 (V) 1960 (Declaration on the Granting of Independence of Colonial Countries and Peoples); Res. 2625 (XXV) (Declaration on the Principles of International Law concerning Friendly Relations).
16. South-West Africa case, ICJ-report 1962; Namibia-case, ICJ-report 1971; Western Sahara-case, ICJ-report 1975.
17. On the history of the Jewish diaspora and the differences it established see e.g. Potok (1989), *Wanderings*, Ballantine Books, New York.
18. In an interview the Dutch Secretary of State for Education, M.J. Cohen, said as much when questioned on his feelings towards being Jewish. He stated that while he did not think about being Jewish that much and his origins were much more in the social democratic movement, he acknowledged he never felt 'not-Jewish' and he always felt deeply affected by what happened to and in Israel, even though he was not a genuine supporter of Israel's policies towards the Palestinians. Ornstein, Van Weezel, Job Cohen laat zich niet kennen, *Vrij Nederland*, 19 March 1994.
19. The Treaty of Maastricht inserted a new article 8 in the EC-Treaty granting the citizenship of the Union to every person holding the nationality of a member state.
20. For obvious reasons, the answer to the question which collective vice applies to the Dutch is left to the imagination of the reader.
21. The imaginary line between North and South should not be attached to states in the legal sense. Roughly drawn, this line starts somewhere south of Great Britain, then going north, cutting the Netherlands in two parts, whereafter it follows the Rhine south again until heading east along the Danube while cutting through Germany.
22. Garreau (1981), *The nine nations of North America*, Avon Books, New York.
23. Case C-379/87, Anita Groener vs Minister for Education and the City of Dublin Vocational Education Committee, [1989] ECR 3967.

Bibliography

Barents, R. (1993), Milieu en interne markt, *Sociaal Economische Wetgeving (SEW)*, 5-29.

Baehr, R., Van Hoof, G.J.H. (1993), Burgerschap en mensenrechten in Hellingman, K. (ed.), *Europa in de steigers: van Gemeenschap tot Unie*, Kluwer, Deventer.

Betten, L. (1985), *The right to strike in Community Law*, North Holland, The Hague.

Bekkers, V.J.J.M., Bonnes, J.M., De Moor-van Vugt, A.J.C., Voermans, W.J.M. (1993), *Brussel en Nederland, tegenliggers, spookrijders of reisgenoten, Implementatie van EG-regelingen in de Nederlandse rechtsorde*, Schoordijk Instituut, W.E.J. Tjeenk Willink, Zwolle.

Bieber, R., Jaque, J.-J., Weiler, J., (eds.) (1985), *An ever closer Union, A critical analysis of the Draft Treaty establishing the European Union*, European University Institute, Florence.

Bleeker, K.A.M. (1993), Verantwoorde communautaire sanctionering van het gemeenschapsrecht, *Nederlands Juristenblad*, 1009-1013.

Borman, T.C. (ed.) (1993), *Aanwijzingen voor de regelgeving*, Staatsdrukkerij en Staatsuitgeverij (SDU), Den Haag.

Brinkhorst, L.J. (1991), Subsidiarity and European Environmental Policy, in *Subsidiarity: The Challenge of Change*, European Institute for Public Administration, Maastricht.

Brinkhorst, L.J. (1992), *Subsidiariteit in het milieurecht*, Kluwer, Deventer.

Burrows, F. (1987), *Free Movement in European Community Law*,

Clarendon Press, Oxford.
Cath, I.F.G. (1991), Hebben ondernemingen recht op bescherming van de privésfeer? De zaken Hoechst en Chappell vergeleken, *NJCM-bulletin*, 28.
Commission of the European Communities (1988), *Social Europe, the social dimension of the internal market*, OOPEC, Luxembourg.
Constantinesco, V. (1991), La subsidiarité comme principe constitutionnel de l'integration européenne, *Aussenwirtschaft*, 439.
Crosby, S. (1991), The Single Market and the Rule of Law, *European Law Review*, 451.
Curtin, D. (1990), The province of government, delimiting the direct effect of directives in the common law context, *European Law Review*.
Degimbe, J. (1991), The Social Dimension of the Internal Market and Subsidiarity, in *Subsidiarity: The Challenge of Change*, European Institute of Public Administration, Maastricht.
Delors, J. (1991), The Principle of Subsidiarity: Contribution to the Debate, in *Subsidiarity: The Challenge of Change*, European Institute of Public Administration, Maastricht.
Emiliou, N. (1992), Subsidiarity : An effective barrier against the 'Enterprises of Ambition', *European Law Review*, 383-407.
F.I.D.E.-report (1994), *Le principe de subsidiarité*, Fédération International de droit Européen, Rome.
Ganz, G. (1987), *Quasi-legislation; Recent Developments in Secondary Legislation*, Sweet & Maxwell, London.
Garreau, J. (1981), *The nine nations of North America*, Avon Books, New York.
Gorbey, D. (1993), *Stilstand is vooruitgang. De dialectiek van het Europese integratieproces*, Van Gorkum en Comp, Assen.
High Level Group on the Operation of the Internal Market (1992), *The Internal Market after 1992, Meeting the Challenge* (Sutherland Report), CEC Brussels.
Heukels, T. (1993), Alternatieve implementatietechnieken en art. 189, lid 3 EEG; grondslagen en ontwikkelingen, *Nederlands Tijdschrift voor Bestuursrecht* 93/1, 59-74.
Jacobs, A.T.J.M. (1986), *Het recht op collectief onderhandelen in rechtsvergelijkend en Europees perspectief*, Samsom/H.D. Tjeenk Willink, Alphen a/d Rijn.
Jessurun d'Oliveira, H.U. (1993), Lesbians and Gays and the Free Movement of Persons, in Waaldijk, C. and Clapham, A. (eds.), *Homosexuality, a European Community Issue*, Kluwer, Deventer.
Joliet, R. (1988), Réglementation étatiques anti-concurrentielles et droit

communautaire, *Cahiers de droit communautaire*.

Kapteyn, P.J.G. (1991), Community Law and the Principle of Subsidiarity, *Revue des Affaires européennes*.

Kapteyn, P.J.G. (1993), De complexe rechtsorde van het Unieverdrag: subsidiariteitsbeginsel en nieuwe bevoegdheden in Hellingman, K. (ed.), *Europa in de steigers: van Gemeenschap tot Unie*, Kluwer, Deventer.

Kapteyn, P.J.G., VerLoren van Themaat, P., Gormley, L. (1989), *Introduction to the Law of the European Communities*, Kluwer, Deventer.

Karpenstein, P. (1988), Doppelte Rechtsgrundlagen im Gemeinschaftsrecht, in Hess, G. (ed.), *Rechtsprobleme der Rechtsangleichung*, Europa Institut der Universität des Saarlandes Vorträg, Saarbrücken.

Keus, L.A.D. (1993), Europees privaatrecht, een bonte lappendeken, in *Preadviezen voor de vereniging voor Burgerlijk recht en de Nederlandse vereniging voor Europees recht*, Koninklijke Vermande, Lelystad.

Kranz, J. (1992), La vote dans la pratique du Conceil des Ministres des Communautes européennes, *Revue Trimestrielle de Droit Européen*.

Krauser, H.P. (1991), Das Prinzip begrenzter Ermächtigung in *Gemeinschaftsrecht als Strukturprinzip des EWG-vertrages*, Schriften zum Europäischer Recht, Band II, Berlin.

Van Kreveld, J.H., *Beleidsregels in het recht*, Kluwer, Deventer 1983.

Korte, J. (1989), Institutionele implicaties van de Europese Akte; de Europese Akte en de instellingen van de EG, *Ars Aequi* 38(1989)5.

Ter Kuile, B.H. (1989), *Hoe ver ligt Den Haag nog van Brussel*, Kluwer Deventer.

Ter Kuile, B.H. (1993), Het verband tussen artikel 177 EG, aalscholvers en pursers, *Nederlands Juristenblad*, 1136-1141.

Lasok, D., Stone, P. (1987), *Conflict of Laws in the European Community*, Professional Books, Abingdon.

Lauwaars, R.H., Maarleveld, J.M. (1987), *Harmonisatie van wetgeving in Europese organisaties*, Kluwer, Deventer.

Loman, A., Mortelmans, K.J.M., Post, H.H.G., Watson, S. (1992), *Culture and Community Law before and after Maastricht*, Kluwer, Deventer.

McPherson, James M. (1988), *Battle Cry of Freedom, The Civil War Era*, Oxford University Press, Oxford.

Van der Meulen, B., Steyger, E., Heldeweg, M., Bakker, R., Cobben, R., Tak, A.Q.C. (1991), Bestuursbevoegdheid als bron van recht, *Nederlands Tijdschrift voor Bestuursrecht*, 133-141.

Mok, M.R. (1993), Over aalscholvers en bijscholing van rechters, *Nederlands Juristenblad*, 1244-1245.

De Moor-van Vugt, A.J.C. (1993), Hobbels bij de rechtshandhaving, in Vervaele, J.A.E. (ed.), *Bestuursrechtelijke toepassing en handhaving van gemeenschapsrecht in Nederland*, Kluwer, Deventer.

Morehead Dworkin, T., Steyger, E. (1989), AIDS victims in the European Community and the United States, Are they protected from Unjustified Discrimination?, *Texas International Law Journal*, Vol. 24, no. 2, Spring.

Mortelmans, K.J.M. (1982), Delegatiewetten ter uitvoering van verdragen en met name ter uitvoering van verplichtingen opgelegd door het Europese Gemeenschapsrecht, in *Liber Amicorum J. Mertens de Wilmars*, Kluwer, Antwerpen.

Mortelmans, K.J.M. (1993), De toepassing en handhaving van het gemeenschapsrecht door het nationaal bestuursrecht, in Vervaele, J.A.E. (ed.), *Bestuursrechtelijke toepassing en handhaving van gemeenschapsrecht in Nederland*, Kluwer, Deventer.

Nilsen, R. (1987), *Learebog i arbejdsret*, Kopenhagen.

Notenboom, H. (1988), *Het Europees parlement en de financiën*, Staatsdrukkerij en Staatsuitgeverij (SDU), Den Haag.

Ornstein, L. Van Weezel, M., Job Cohen laat zich niet kennen, *Vrij Nederland*, 19 March 1994.

Pappas S.A. (1991), The Legal Basis for Action to be Taken by the European Community in the Field of Environment in *Subsidiarity: The Challenge of Change*, European Institute for Public Administration, Maastricht.

Pennings, F. (1992), Is the Subsidiarity Principle Useful to Guide the European Integration Process?, *Tilburg Foreign Law Review* 1992/93, Vol. II, Issue 2.

Pescatore, P. (1968), Les droits de l'homme et l'integration européen, *Cahiers de droit européen*, 629-672.

Pescatore, P. (1987), Some critical remarks on the Single European Act, *Common Market Law Review* no. 1.

Pinder, J. (1986), European Community and National State: a case for a neo-federalism, *International affairs*, 41-54.

Philips Eindhoven (1984), *Europe 1990, an agenda for action*, Eindhoven.

Potok, Ch. (1989), *Wanderings*, Ballantine Books, New York.

Prechal, S., Burrows, N. (1990), *Gender Discrimination Law of the European Community*, Darthmouth Publishing Company, Aldershot.

Prechal, S. (1990), Remedies after Marshall, *Common Market Law Review*, Summer.

Prechal, S. (1991), Richtlijnconforme uitleg, Alice in Wonderland, *Weekblad voor Fiscaal Recht*, 1991/5984, 1596.

Rasmussen, H. (1986), *On Law and Policy in the European Court of Justice*, Nijhoff Publishers, Dordrecht.

Van Rijn, Th. (1978), *Exceptie van onwettigheid en prejudiciele procedure inzake geldigheid van gemeenschapsrecht*, Kluwer, Deventer.

Rigeaux, M. (1992), *EEC-competence in the Cultural Field*, Kluwer, Deventer.

Sevenster, H. (1992), *Milieubeleid en gemeenschapsrecht*, Kluwer, Deventer.

Sevinga, K. (1991), EG, Grondrechten en grondwet, *Nederlands Juristenblad*, 1667.

Sewandono, A. (1992), Beginsel van democratie versus milieu, *Nederlands Juristenblad*, 63.

Schröer, T. (1991), Mehr Demokratie statt umweltpolitischen Subsidiarität, *Europarecht*, 356.

Steyger, E. (1990), Vertrouwen is goed, controle is beter; bevoegdheidsoverdracht en democratische controle in pre-federaal Europa, in Heringa, A.W., Verheij, N. (eds.), *Publiekrechtelijke bewegingen*, Kluwer, Deventer.

Steyger, E. (1990), *Medezeggenschap bij veiligheid en gezondheid: de Europese regelingen*, Kluwer, Deventer.

Steyger, E. (1991), De directe toepassing van richtlijnen door anderen dan de Staat, *RegelMaat* no. 1.

Steyger, E. (1991), Holt de interne markt de arbeidsmilieurichtlijnen uit, *Sociaal Economische Wetgeving (SEW)*, 616-620.

Steyger, E. (1992), Eenwording door versnippering, de overeenkomst betreffende de Europese economische ruimte, *RegelMaat*, 1992-4, 94.

Steyger, E. (1993), European Community Law and the self-regulatory Capacity of Society, *Journal of Common Market Studies*, Volume 31, no. 2, June.

Steyger, E. (1993), Nogmaals over 177 EG, aalscholvers en pursers, *Nederlands Juristenblad*, 1482-1483.

Steyger, E. (1994), Het Europese recht en nationale systemen van sociale zekerheid, *Sociaal Maandblad Arbeid*, Volume 49, 1 and 2.

Temple Lang, J. (1990), Community Constitutional Law: Article 5 EEC-Treaty, *27 Common Market Law Review*, 645.

Temple Lang, J. (1991), The Sphere in which Member States are obliged to comply with the General Principles of Law and Community Fundamental Rights Principles, *Legal Issues of European Integration*, 1991/2, p. 2335.

Timmermans, C.W.A. (1980), Harmonisatie van wetgeving en Nederlands recht; beeld van bewogen beweging, *R.M. Themis*, 406-431.

Tribe, Laurence H. (1988), *American Constitutional Law*, Mineola, New York.

Tribe, Laurence H. (1992), *Abortion, the Clash of Absolutes*, Norton and Company, New York.

Usher, J.A. (1981), *European Community Law and National Law, The irreversible transfer*, Sweet and Maxwell, Londen.

Verbraeken, E. (1993), Dicatuur van het gemeenschapsrecht, *Nederlands Juristenblad*, 1483-1484.

Verheij, N. (1990), Naar een wetboek van bestuursrecht, in Verheij, N., Heringa, A.W. (eds.), *Publiekrechtelijke bewegingen*, Kluwer, Deventer.

Vervaele J.A.E. (ed.) (1993), *Bestuursrechtelijke toepassing en handhaving van gemeenschapsrecht in Nederland*, Kluwer, Deventer.

Vervaele, J.A.E. (1993), Administrative sanctiebevoegdheden van en in de Gemeenschap. Naar een systeem van administrative bestuurssancties?, in Vervaele. J.A.E. (ed.), *Bestuursrechtelijke toepassing en handhaving van gemeenschapsrecht in Nederland*, Kluwer, Deventer.

Vervaele, J.A.E. (1994), *Handen en tanden van het Gemeenschapsrecht, beschouwingen over publieke rechtshandhaving*, Kluwer, Deventer.

Lord Wedderburn (1986), *The Worker and the Law*, Penguin Books, Harmondsworth.

Wellens, K.C., Borchardt, G.M. (1989), Soft Law in European Community Law, *European Law Review*, 267-321.

De Witte, B. (1991), Community Law and National Constitutional Values, *Legal Issues of European Integration*, 1991/2, 1-22.

Wolters, M. (1992), Steen der wijzen ontbreekt bij subsidiariteitsbeginsel, *Official Journal of the Netherlands*, 222.

Wilke, M., Wallace, H. (1990), *Subsidiarity: Approaches to Power-sharing in the European Community*, RIIA discussion papers no. 27, London.

De Zwaan, J.W. (1986), The Single European Act, Conclusion of a Unique Document, *Common Market Law Review*.

Table of Cases

Cases are listed in chronological order

8/55	Fédération Charbonnière de Belgique vs High Authority, [1954-1956] ECR 245
9/56	Meroni vs High Authority, [1957 and 1958] ECR 133
10/56	Meroni vs High Authority, [1957 and 1958] ECR 157
1/58	Stork vs High Authority, [1959] ECR 17
36-38, 40/59	'Präsident', 'Geitling', 'Mausegatt' and I Nold vs High Authority, [1960] ECR 423
26/62	Van Gend en Loos vs Nederlandse administratie der belastingen, [1963] ECR 1
6/64	Costa vs ENEL, [1964] ECR 585
20/64	Albatros vs Sopeco, [1965] ECR 1
40/64	Marcello Scarlate et al. vs Commission, [1965] ECR 215
61/65	Weduwe Vaassen vs Bestuur Beambtenfonds Mijnbedrijf, [1965] ECR 257
14/68	Wilhelm et al. vs Bundeskartellamt, [1969] ECR 1
29/69	Erich Stauder vs Stadt Ulm Socialamt, [1969] ECR 419
40/69	Hauptzollamt Hamburg-Oberelbe vs Fa. Bollmann, [1970] ECR 69
74/69	Hauptzollamt Bremen-Freihafen vs Waren-Import-Gesellschaft Krohn, [1970] ECR 451
11/70	Internationale Handelsgesellschaft, [1970] ECR 1125
22/70	Commission vs Council, [1971] ECR 263 at 274-276

25/70	Einfuhr und Vorratstelle für Getreide und Futtermittel vs Köster, [1970] ECR 1161
78/70	Deutsche Gramofon Gesellschaft GmbH vs Metro-SB-Grossmarkte, [1971] ECR 487
80/70	Defrenne vs Sabena I, [1971] ECR 445
7/71	Commission vs France, [1971] ECR 1003
6/72	Continental Can, [1973] ECR 215
39/72	Commission vs Italy, [1973] ECR 101
4/73	J. Nold vs Commission, [1974] ECR 491
2/74	Reyners vs Belgian State, [1974] ECR 631
8/74	Procureur du Roi vs Dassonville et al., [1974] ECR 837
36/74	Walrave and Koch vs Association Union Cycliste Internationale, [1974] ECR 1405
41/74	Yvonne van Duyn vs Home Office, [1974] ECR 1337
9/75	Meyer-Burckhardt, [1975] ECR 1171
23/75	Rey Soda, [1975] ECR 1279
43/75	Gabrielle Defrenne vs Sabena Airlines II, [1976] ECR 455
59/75	Manghera, [1976] ECR 91
33/76	Rewe Zentralfinanz and Rewe Zentral AG vs Landwirtschaftskammer für das Saarland, [1976] ECR 1989
35/76	Simmenthal, [1976] ECR 1871
41/76	Donckerwolcke et al. vs Procureur de la Republique et al., [1976] ECR 1921
50/76	Amsterdam Bulb BV vs Produktschap voor Siergewassen, [1977] ECR 137
51/76	Verbond van Nederlandse Ondernemingen vs Inspecteur der Invoerrechten en Accijnzen, [1977] ECR 113
90/76	SRL Ufficio Henry van Ameyde vs SRL Ufficio Centrale Italiano, [1977] ECR 1091
30/77	Regina vs Bouchereau, [1977] ECR 1999
38/77	ENKA BV vs Inspecteur der Invoerrechten en Accijnzen, [1977] ECR 2203
94/77	Fratelli Zerbone vs Amministrazione delle Fianze della Stato, [1978] ECR 99
106/77	Simmenthal II, [1978] ECR 629
16/78	Choquet, [1978] ECR 2293
92/78	Simmenthal SpA vs Commission, [1979] ECR 777
110-1/78	Van Wesemael, [1979] ECR 35
120/78	Cassis de Dijon, [1979] 649
148/78	Publicco Ministero vs Ratti, [1979] ECR 1629
32/79	Commission vs United Kingdom, [1980] ECR 2403 at 2434
44/79	Hauer vs Rheinland-Pfalz, [1979] ECR 3727

52/79	Debauve, [1980] ECR 833
61/79	Amministrazione delle Finanze della Stato vs Denkavit Italiana Srl., [1980] ECR 1205
62/79	SA Compagnie generale pour la Diffusion de la Television Coditel et al. vs SA Cine Vog Films et al., [1980] ECR 881
68/79	Hans Just vs Danish Ministry for Fiscal Affairs, [1980] ECR 501
136/79	National Panasonic, [1980] ECR 2033
138/79	Roquette, [1980] ECR 3333
139/79	Maizena, [1980] ECR 3393
804/79	Commission vs United Kingdom, [1981] ECR 1045
69/80	Worringham vs Lloyds Bank Ltd, [1981] ECR 767
98/80	Romano vs Institut National d'Assurance Maladie Invalidité, [1981] ECR 1241
246/80	C. Broekmeulen vs Huisartsen registratie commissie, [1981] ECR 2311
279/80	Webb, [1981] ECR 3320
8/81	Becker vs Finanzamt Münster Innenstadt, [1983] ECR 53
12/81	Garland vs British Rail, [1982] ECR 359
53/81	Levin, [1982] ECR 1035
91/81	Commission vs Italy, [1982] ECR 2133
96/81	Commission vs The Netherlands, [1982] ECR 1791
97/81	Commission vs The Netherlands, [1982] ECR 1819
115-6/81	Adoui and Cornuaille vs Belgium, [1982] ECR 1665
213-5/81	Norddeutsches Vieh und Fleischkontor Herbert Will et al. vs Bundesanstalt für Landeswirtschaftliche Marktordnung, [1982] ECR 3583
262/81	Coditel II, [1982] ECR 3381
300/81	Commission vs Italian Republic, [1983] ECR 449
35-6/82	Morson and Jhanjan, [1982] ECR 3723
174/82	Sandoz, [1983] ECR 2445
199/82	Amministrazione delle Finanze dello Stato vs San Georgio SpA, [1983] ECR 3595
227/82	Van Bennekom, [1983] ECR 3883
286/82 & 26/83	Luisi & Carbone vs Ministero del Tesoro, [1984] ECR 377
13/83	European Parliament vs Council, [1985] ECR 1513
14/83	Von Colson and Kamann vs Land Nordrhein West-Falen, [1984] ECR 1891
19/83	Wendelboe, [1985] ECR 457
47-8/83	Pluimveeslachterij Midden Nederland BV et al., [1984] ECR 721 at 1738

79/83	Harz vs Deutsche Tradax, [1984] ECR 1921
143/83	Commission vs Denmark, [1985] ECR 427
215/83	Commission vs Belgium, [1985] ECR 1039
267/83	Diatta vs Land Berlin, [1985] ECR 567
293/83	Gravier vs City of Liege, [1985] ECR 593
29/84	Commission vs Germany, [1985] ECR 1661
105/84	Mikkelsen vs Danmols, [1985] ECR 2639
152/84	Marshall vs Southampton and South West Health Authority, [1986] ECR 723
222/84	Johnston vs Royal Ulster Constabulary, [1986] ECR 1651
235/84	Commission vs Italy, [1986] ECR 2291
59/85	The Netherlands vs Ann Florence Reed, [1986] ECR 1283
71/85	FNV vs The Netherlands, [1986] ECR 3855
139/85	Kempf, [1986] ECR 1741
239/85	Commission vs Belgium, [1986] ECR 3645
311/85	Vlaamse reisbureau's, [1987] ECR 3801
314/85	Foto-Frost vs. Hauptzollamt Lübeck-Ost, [1987] ECR 4199
325/85	Ireland vs Commission, [1987] ECR 5041
352/85	Bond van Adverteerders, [1988] ECR 2085
429/85	Commission vs Italy, [1988] ECR 843
12/86	Demirel, [1987] ECR 3719
24/86	Blaizot vs City of Liege et al., [1988] ECR 379
45/86	Commission vs Council, [1987] ECR 1493
68/86	United Kingdom vs Council, [1988] ECR 855
80/86	Kolpinghuis, [1987] ECR 3969
126/86	Giminez Zaera vs Instituto Nacional de la Seguridad Social and Tesoria General de la Seguridad Social, [1987] ECR 3697
131/86	United Kingdom vs Council, [1988] ECR 905
222/86	Heylens, [1987] ECR 4097
267/86	Van Eycke, [1988] ECR 4769
316/86	Jonas vs Krücken, [1988] ECR 2213
22/87	Commission vs Italy, [1989] ECR 143
31/87	Gebroeders Beentjes, [1988] ECR 4635
46/87 & 227/88	Hoechst, [1989] ECR 2859
C-131/87	Commission vs United Kingdom and Denmark, [1989] ECR 3743
165/87	Commission vs Council, [1988] ECR 5545
186/87	Cowan, [1989] ECR 195
204/87	Bekaert, [1988] ECR 2029
242/87	Commission vs Council, [1989] ECR 1425

275/87 Commission vs Council, [1989] ECR 259
C-339/87 Commission vs The Netherlands, [1990] ECR I-851
C-379/87 Anita Groener vs Minister for Education and the City of Dublin Vocational Education Committee, [1989] ECR 3967
380/87 Enichem Base c.s. vs Comune di Cinisello Balsamo, [1989] ECR 2491
C-11/88 Commission vs Council, [1989] ECR 3799
C-16/88 Commission vs Council, [1989] ECR 3457
C-56/88 United Kingdom vs Council, [1989] ECR 1615
C-62/88 Greece vs Council, [1990] ECR 1527
C-68/88 Commission vs Greece, [1989] ECR 2965
C-70/88 European Parliament vs Council, [1990] ECR I-2041
C-103/88 Fratelli Constanzo vs Commune di Milano, [1989] ECR 1839
C-109/88 Danfoss, [1989] ECR 3199
C-177/88 Dekker vs Stichting Vormingswerk Jong Volwassenen, [1990] ECR I-3941
C-262/88 Barber vs Guardian Royal Exchange Assurance Group, [1990] ECR 1889
C-331/88 FEDESA, [1990] ECR 4023
C-361/88 Commission vs Germany, [1991] ECR I-2567
C-369/88 Delattre, [1991] ECR 1487
C-14/89 Nino et al., [1990] ECR 3537
C-51/89 & C-90/89 & C-94/89 United Kingdom vs Council, [1991] ECR I-2757
C-58/89 Commission vs Germany, 17-10-1991, [1991] ECR I-2607
C-106/89 Marleasing, [1990] ECR I-4135
C-154/89 Commission vs France, [1990] ECR I-659
C-188/89 Foster vs British Gas Plc, [1990] ECR I-3313
C-198/89 Commission vs Greece, [1991] ECR I-727
C-213/89 Factortame vs Secretary of State for Transport, [1990] ECR 2433
C-260/89 ERT, [1991] ECR 2925
C-300/89 Commission supported by the European Parliament vs Council, [1991] ECR 2867
C-348/89 Menacarte-Metalurgica da Lagao Lda. vs Chefe do Serviço da Conferencia Final da Alfandega do Porto, 27-6-1991, [1991] ECR I-3277
C-377/89 Cotter and McDermott vs Minister for Social Welfare and Attorney General, [1991] ECR I-1155
C-6/90 Andrea Francovich and Daniela Bonifaci vs Italian Republic,

& C-9/90	[1991] ECR I-5357
C-13/90 & C-14/90 & C-64/90	Commission vs France, [1991] ECR nyr
C-46/90 & C-93/91	J.-M. Lagauche, 27 October 1993, [1993] ECR nyr
C-76/90	Säger vs Dennemeyer, [1990] ECR I-4221
C-159/90	S.P.U.C. vs Grogan, [1991] ECR 4685
C-208/90	Theresa Emmott vs the Minister for Social Welfare and the Attorney General, 25-7-1991, [1991] ECR nyr
C-240/90	Germany vs Commission, 27-10-1992, [1992] ECR nyr
C-295/90	European Parliament vs Council, 7-7-1992, [1992] ECR nyr
C-332/90	V. Steen vs Deutsche Bundespost, 28-1-1992, [1992] ECR nyr
C-369/90	Micheletti vs Delegación del Gobierno en Cantabria, 7-7-1992, [1992] ECR nyr
C-29/91	Sophie Redmond Stichting vs H. Bartol, 19-5-1992, [1992] ECR nyr
C-148/91	Vereniging Veronica Omroep Organisatie vs Commissariaat voor de Media, 3-2-1993, [1993] ECR nyr
C-155/91	Commission, supported by the European Parliament vs Council, 17-3-1993, [1993] ECR nyr
C-159/91 & 160/91	Poucet vs AGF et Camulrac and Pistre vs Cancave, [1993] ECR nyr
C-267/91 & 268/91	Keck and Mithouard, [1993] ECR nyr
C-271/91	Marshall vs Southampton and South West Hampshire Area Health Authority II, [1993] ECR nyr
C-338/91	Steenhorst-Neerings, 27-10-1993, [1993] ECR nyr
C-11/92	R. vs Secretary of State for Health, *ex parte* Gallagher, [1993] ECR nyr
C-17/92	Federación de Distribuidores Cinematográficos (FEDECINE) vs Spain, [1993] ECR nyr
C-93/92	CMC Motorradcenter GmbH vs Baskiciogullari, 13-10-1993, [1993] ECR nyr
C-127/92	P.M. Enderby vs Frenchay Health Authority (FHA), 27-10-1993, [1993] ECR nyr
C-188/92	TWD Textilwerke Deggendorf vs Germany, pending
C-240/92	Germany vs Commission, [1992] ECR nyr
C-292/92	Hünermund vs Landesapothekerkammer Baden-Würtemberg, [1993] ECR nyr
C-46/93	Brasserie du pêcheur SA vs Federal Republic of Germany,

	pending
C-48/93	Factortame III, pending
C-61/93	Commission vs the Netherlands, [1994] ECR nyr
C-327/93	R. vs Secretary of State for National Heritage, *ex parte* Continental Television BVio et al., pending
C-430/93	Van Schijndel vs Pensioenfonds voor Fysiotherapeuten, pending
C-13/94	P. vs S. and Cornwall County Council, pending
C-194/94	SA C.I.A. Security International vs SA Signalson SPRL Securitel, pending

Opinion 1/76, [1977] ECR 741

Opinion of the Court of Justice on ILO-treaty nr 170, 2/91 OJ 1993 C-109/1

Opinion of the Court of Justice on the competence of the Commission to conclude the WTO-Agreements, 1/94, 15 November 1994, [1994] ECR nyr

Index